BOURNEMC

TROLLEYBUSES

Malcolm N Pearce

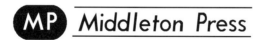

MP *Middleton Press*

Published May 1998
First reprint April 1999
Second reprint June 2003

ISBN 1 901706 10 9

© Middleton Press, 1998

Design Deborah Esher

Published by
        Middleton Press
        Easebourne Lane
        Midhurst, West Sussex
        GU29 9AZ
Tel: 01730 813169
Fax: 01730 812601
Email: enquiries@middletonpress.fsnet.co.uk

Printed & bound by Biddles Ltd, Kings Lynn

CONTENTS

INTRODUCTION AND ACKNOWLEDGEMENTS

I was still a teenager when the last trolleybuses were withdrawn from regular service in Bournemouth. As one whose youth was preoccupied by a growing interest in music I was, alas, inattentive to the minutiae of a method of tranport that I took very much for granted. However, I do cherish clear memories of the trolleys that purred their way effortlessly up the incline of Beaufort Road to take me from my childhood home in West Southbourne to Fisherman's Walk, Boscombe and beyond. I also remember being puzzled as to why this "silent service" should have been abandoned in favour of the diesel buses that seemed to shake the very foundations of our later family home in Holdenhurst Road.

Although a teacher by profession (I am Director of Music at Magdalen College School, Oxford) my pedigree in the transport history of Bournemouth is a strong one. My paternal grandfather, Percy, came to Bournemouth in 1906 as a clerk to the Transport Manager, a post he held under four incumbents until his retirement in 1947. Thus my father, Gordon, was raised with a strong interest in the public transport system. He claimed to have been the first member of the general public to travel on a trolleybus in Bournemouth having obtained permission from the General Manager to ride on a midnight trial run of the experimental single-deck "Bluebird".

He subsequently chronicled the development and decline of the trolleybus system over the next 36 years recording on film many of the significant events. His account of the Bournemouth tram and bus system which appeared in Buses Illustrated in January 1952 was among the very first to be published. In 1956 his passionate advocacy of the electrically powered bus won a prize in an essay competition run by the British Electrical and Allied Manufacturers Association. At the same time his cogent defence of this method of transport through the correspondence columns of the local press at a time when its continuance was under threat earned him an unsolicited letter of appreciation from the General Manager, Mr Reakes.

As I have discovered to my benefit, students of the history of Bournemouth's bus system are admirably served by an excellent fund of literature, principally John Mawson's comprehensive account (1967) and authoritative booklets by David Chalk (1962, 1969 & 1977) and W.P.Ransom (1982). I am very grateful to those who have given me help and encouragement and who have permitted me generous access to their collections of material, especially David Chalk, John Clifford, Richard Sinclair, Graham Teasdill, Philip Thomas and my editor Robert Harley. To Gay Sturt, another Bournemouthian exiled to Oxford, I am grateful for help in matters photographic. Above all I am indebted to my late father for his foresight in gathering together such an abundant archive of material concerning Bournemouth's trolleybuses. To his memory this book is affectionately dedicated.

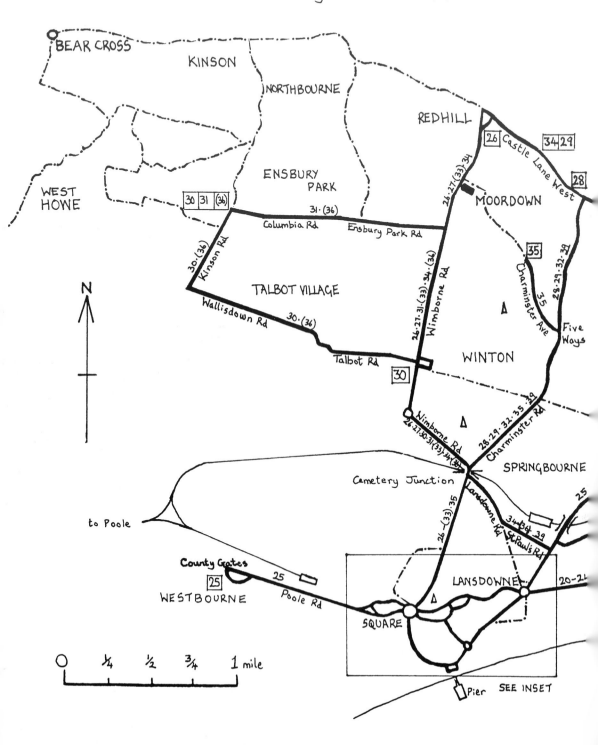

BOURNEMOUTH CORPORATION TRANSPORT
TROLLEYBUS SYSTEM showing routes as at 1963-1964

BEAR CROSS

KINSON

NORTHBOURNE

REDHILL

26 Castle Lane West   34 29

28

WEST HOWE

ENSBURY PARK

30 31 (36)

31·(36)

Columbia Rd

Ensbury Park Rd

26·27·(33) 34

MOORDOWN

35

28·29·32·39

30·(36)

Kinson Rd

TALBOT VILLAGE

Wallisdown Rd

30·(36)

26·27·31·(33)·34·(36)

Wimborne Rd

Charminster Ave

35

Five Ways

Talbot Rd

30

WINTON

Wimborne Rd

26·27·30·31·(33)·34·(36)

28·29·32·35·39

Charminster Rd

Cemetery Junction

SPRINGBOURNE

25

to Poole

26·(33)·35

Lansdowne Rd

34·(36)·39

St Paul's Rd

County Gates   25

25

Poole Rd

LANSDOWNE

20·21

WESTBOURNE

SQUARE

Pier   SEE INSET

N

¼   ½   ¾   1 mile

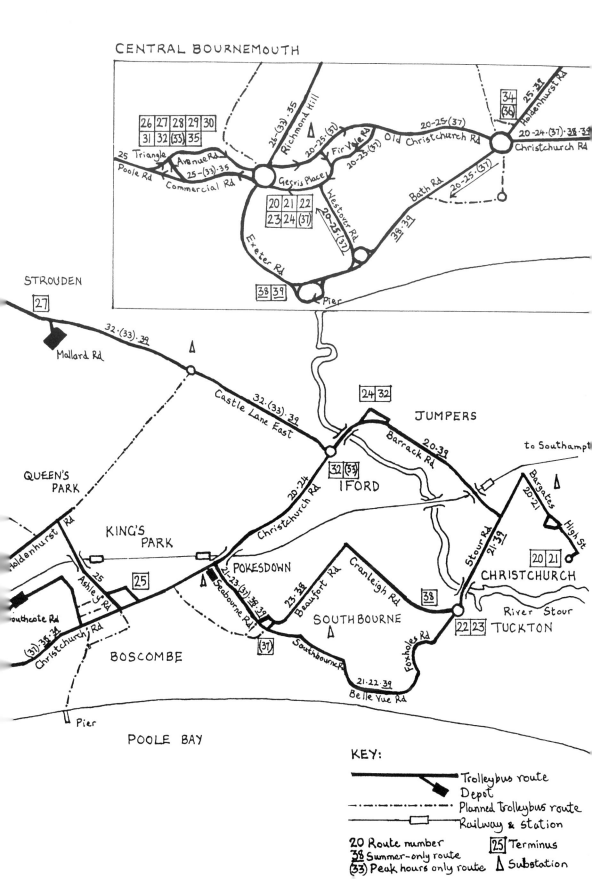

CENTRAL BOURNEMOUTH

| 26 | 27 | 28 | 29 | 30 |
| 31 | 32 | (33) | 35 | |

25 Triangle
Poole Rd
Avenue Rd
25-(33)-35
Commercial Rd
Gervis Place
Richmond Hill
26-(33)-35
20-25-(50)
Fir Vale Rd
20-25-(37)
Old Christchurch Rd
20-25-(37)
25-39

| 34 |
| (36) |
Holdenhurst Rd

20-24-(37)-38-39
Christchurch Rd

| 20 | 21 | 22 |
| 23 | 24 | (37) |
20-25-(37)
Westover Rd
Exeter Rd
Bath Rd
20-25-(37)
38-39

| 38 | 39 |
Pier

STROUDEN

| 27 |

32-(33)-39
Mallard Rd

Castle Lane East
32-(33)-39

| 24 | 32 |

JUMPERS

Barrack Rd
20-39

to Southampton

QUEEN'S PARK

20-24
Christchurch Rd

| 32 | (33) |
IFORD

Bargates
20-21
High St

| 20 | 21 |
CHRISTCHURCH

Stour Rd
21-39

KING'S PARK

Holdenhurst Rd

| 25 |
Ashley Rd
Southcote Rd
(37)-38-39
Christchurch Rd

POKESDOWN
Seabourne Rd
21-23-(37)-38-39

Beaufort Rd
Cranleigh Rd
23-38

| 38 |

SOUTHBOURNE

River Stour

| 22 | 23 |
TUCKTON

BOSCOMBE

| 37 |
Southbourne Rd

Foxholes Rd

21-22-39
Belle Vue Rd

Pier

POOLE BAY

KEY:

— Trolleybus route
◆ Depot
–·–·– Planned trolleybus route
▭ Railway & station

20 Route number
38 Summer-only route
(33) Peak hours only route

25 Terminus
△ Substation

GEOGRAPHICAL SETTING

During the trolleybus era the Borough of Bournemouth was part of the county of Hampshire, the western limits of its transport system abutting the neighbouring Borough of Poole in Dorset at County Gates and Wallisdown. This seaside resort enjoys a raised clifftop location overlooking Poole Bay, the sands and gravels upon which it is situated being dissected by dry valleys, known locally as Chines where they reach to the coast. The only watercourse is the Bourne stream whose valley is the focal point of the town centre and out of which routes climb steeply. Along the north eastern perimeter of the town the land descends to the valley of the River Stour on the far side of which, at the edge of the harbour formed by its confluence with the Hampshire Avon, lies the ancient Borough of Christchurch.

HISTORICAL BACKGROUND

Bournemouth's interest in the "trackless tram" dates back to the earliest days of its deployment in this country. A number of local schemes predate the First World War but never came to fruition. In 1922 interest was rekindled when Bournemouth was host to the Tramways and Light Railways Congress. It was here that Trackless Cars of Leeds exhibited a 64-seater trolleybus, demonstrating its operation at the Southcote Road depot. In 1928 Poole, whose tramways had been operated by Bournemouth Corporation under a lease agreement since 1905, obtained authority to operate "omnibuses moved by electrical power". This authority was never put into action nor, interestingly, did Poole ever permit Bournemouth to operate trolleybuses over their territory when, two years later, the Bournemouth Corporation Act (1930) came into being. The Act gave powers for trolleybuses to operate over all tram routes, extant or authorised, as well as new routes.

Action was not immediate; it was not until May 1933 that an experimental route was set up. The chosen route, between the Square and Westbourne, was equipped with poles and wires and four vehicles of various types hired. The scheme quickly proved to be a success and the decision was made to convert to trolleybus operation over a period of three years. Confirmation of the favourable economics of trolleybuses relative to other motor vehicles was provided by figures from Wolverhampton, which had built up an extensive system over the previous decade. The experimental route was therefore extended up to the Lansdowne and along Holdenhurst and Ashley Roads to Boscombe. It passed near to the main depot at Southcote Road, access to which was provided both from the Central Station and Boscombe ends.

Route 25 was opened on 22nd June 1934 by Lt. Col. C. M. Headlam, Parliamentary Secretary to the Minister of Transport. Further development was swift. Within the next two years the trolley wires had reached along Christchurch Road to Iford (route 24) and extended out of the Square up Richmond Hill, the "side road" routes, as they were known, radiating from Cemetery Junction towards the Central Station (route 27), Charminster Road (route 26) and through Winton to the Moordown Depot (route 28). Additions, made in 1937, provided a short spur from Five Ways up Charminster Avenue (route 29) and an alternative route from Lansdowne to the Square via Bath and Westover Roads.

Progress from Pokesdown towards Christchurch was accomplished in three stages. The wires reached Fisherman's Walk (route 23) in November and then Southbourne Cross Roads (route 22) in December 1935. Christchurch Corporation had stipulated that the tram service from the Square to Christchurch should remain intact until the entire trolleybus route had been installed. Thus it was not until the final stretch of line had been completed and route 21 opened with due ceremony on 8th April 1936 that the trams finally quitted the scene. Proposals were now put forward for several new routes and were confirmed by the Bournemouth Corporation (Trolley Vehicles) Act, 1938. Some of these schemes were ambitious and, along with a few remaining from the 1930 Act, were never realised. However, routes 30 (via Talbot Road) and 30a (via Ensbury Park Road) to Wallisdown were completed before hostilities broke out in 1939.

Whilst Bournemouth was never a primary target for enemy bombs the town centre was not entirely immune to the attentions of the Luftwaffe. Damage caused by raids necessitated the erection of a turning circle at Horseshoe Common and a temporary diversion in the Square. In emergency, buses were turned using a T-pole at the top of Richmond Hill. Over thirty vehicles were loaned to other undertakings, principally Wolverhampton and Ilford. However, the development of the system did not come to a complete halt. In 1943 the lines were extended across Iford Bridge and along Barrack Road to the junction with Stour Road (route 20).

Post-war austerity brought both benefits and frustrations for the trolleybus. Electrically-powered transport proved popular at a time when fuel for the internal-combustion engine was rationed. However, materials for developing new routes were in short supply and the final additions to the system were accomplished slowly. Fisherman's Walk to Tuckton via Cranleigh Road (route 22b) was opened in 1948 and the long-planned lines to Bournemouth Pier opened on Good Friday 1950. Finally, the route along Castle Lane, commenced pre-war but only completed between Moordown and Broadway, was finished in 1951. Work had commenced on the new depot at Mallard Road and the first phase of this innovative and impressive structure was completed in 1953.

At its zenith the Bournemouth trolleybus system consisted of just over 29 route miles and was as extensive as many other large undertakings (London excluded) even if the fleet was not as sizeable as those which were obliged to operate more intensive services. In the latest vehicles, delivered in 1950, the comfort of the passenger was paramount. Luxurious, well-spaced seating was served by a rear entrance / front exit system that ensured easy movement of passengers. The system as a whole was remarkably safe and efficient. The incident, which occurred in December 1950, when two buses collided in icy conditions at Stokewood Road was very rare indeed, as was the immobilisation of the entire system due to a freak storm in August 1955. In 1953 the trolleys carried forty million passengers over three million route miles, the surplus generated by their revenue cancelling out the deficit caused by motor-bus operation.

Nonetheless, uncertainties began to surface. The threat of nationalisation, rising costs of generating electricity relative to the cost of diesel fuel and doubts concerning the range and manoeuvrability of such vehicles on the increasingly congested roads caused debate. Balanced against this was the high expectation at that time that developments in the field of nuclear energy would soon yield a good source of cheap electricity. In the meantime, though, the advent of the new power station (now demolished) at Poole enabled the undertaking's ageing generating plant at Southcote Road to be decommissioned in 1955. From August 31st of that year all electrical current was supplied to the system by the Southern Electricity Board via eight substations.

The renumbering of routes which took place in 1956 eliminated the use of letter suffixes to route numbers. The acquisition in 1958 of new, speedier two-axle vehicles to replace superannuated stock necessitated a renumbering of the fleet. As late as 1962 plans were well in hand to complete the link between the Queen's Park terminus and Castle Lane. But nine new vehicles delivered that year proved to be the last trolleybuses supplied to a British operator. The hard winter of 1962-63 demonstrated the system's vulnerability under such circumstances. The decision, taken early in 1963, that no more trolleys would be ordered signalled the beginning of the end.

It was the redevelopment of the road system in the Central Station and St. Paul's Road area that caused the withdrawal of some minor services later in 1963. The main bulk of the conversion of trolley routes began in 1965 and by Autumn 1966 all the "side road" routes were being operated by diesel buses. Ironically, conversion of the "main road" routes (nos 20 - 24) planned for 1968 was postponed by delays in the delivery of replacement diesel vehicles. The last timetabled services ran on 19th April 1969 and the final procession of trolleybuses from the Pier to Mallard Road via Christchurch took place the next day.

1. For trolleys arriving at County Gates the one-way system round the crescent of Seamoor Road and part of Poole Road provided a natural turning point. British United Traction 200, on its first day in service in October 1950, is admired by a clutch of small boys as it waits in Seamoor Road before setting off on the return journey towards Boscombe.   (G.O.P.Pearce)

October 1953 timetable

SERVICE 25. Westbourne—Queen's Park (Golf Pavilion)
SERVICE 25a. Westbourne—Ashley Road, Boscombe
via West Station, Square, Lansdowne, Central Station, Capstone Road and Queen's Park

WEEKDAYS

		am	am	am	am	am	am	am		pm	pm	pm
WESTBOURNE ...	dep.	...	6 2	6 22	6 42	7 2	7 12	7 22	then every	10 58	11 6	11 14
SQUARE ...	,,	5 50	6 10	6 30	6 50	7 10	7 20	7 30	few	11 6	11 13	11 21
Central Station ...	,,	5 57	6 17	6 37	6 57	7 17	7 27	7 37	minutes	11 13	11 20	11 28
ASHLEY ROAD ...	arr.	6 6	6 26	6 46	7 6	7 26	7 36	7 46	until	11 22	...	

		am	am	am	am	am	am	am	am		pm	pm
ASHLEY ROAD ...	dep.	5 36	5 56	6 16	6 36	6 50	...	...	7 10	then every	10 39	10 47
Central Station ...	,,	5 46	6 6	6 26	6 46	6 58	...	...	7 20	few	10 49	10 57
SQUARE ...	,,	5 53	6 13	6 33	6 53	7 5	7 13	7 21	7 29	minutes	10 57	11 5
WESTBOURNE ...	arr.	6 0	6 20	6 40	7 0	7 10	7 20	7 28	7 36	until	11 4	11 12

Service 25 Buses leave Square for Queen's Park 8.22, 9.4 a.m., then every 30 mins. until 7.4, 8.2, 9.6, 10.2 p.m.
Queen's Park for Westbourne 8.44, 9.26, a.m., then every 30 mins. until 7.26, 8.26, 9.30, 10.26 p.m.

SUNDAYS

		am	am	am	am	am	then	pm	pm	then	pm	then	pm	pm	pm
WESTBOURNE ...	dep.	...	...	9 10	...	9 36	every 10 mins. until	12 6	12 26	every few mins. until	7 45	every 10 mins. until	10 25	10 35	10 45
SQUARE ...	,,	7 30	8 15	9 15	9 34	9 44		12 14	12 36		7 53		10 33	10 43	10 53
Central Station ...	,,	7 35	8 20	9 20	9 42	9 52		12 22	12 44		8 1		10 40	10 50	11 0
ASHLEY ROAD ...	arr.	7 40	8 25	9 25	9 50	10 0		12 30	12 53		8 9		10 49	...	...

		am	am	am	am	am	am	then	pm	then	pm	then	pm	pm	pm
ASHLEY ROAD ...	dep.	...	7 40	8 0	8 45	...	9 20	every 10 mins. until	12 0	every few mins. until	7 19	every 10 mins. until	10 9	10 19	10 29
Central Station ...	,,	6 55	7 47	8 7	8 52	...	9 29		12 9		7 28		10 18	10 28	10 38
SQUARE ...	,,	7 2	7 55	8 15	9 0	9 28	9 38		12 18		7 37		10 27	10 37	10 47
WESTBOURNE ...	arr.	...	...	...	9 7	9 35	9 45		12 25		7 44		10 34	10 44	...

Service 25 Buses leave Square for Queen's Park 10.24 a.m., 12.30, 1.0, 1.32, 1.56, 2.36, 3.0, 3.32, 4.4, 4.36, 5.0, 5.32, 5.56, 6.36 p.m.
Queen's Park for Westbourne 10.43 a.m., 12.45, 1.25, 1.57, 2.20, 3.1, 3.25, 3.57, 4.29, 5.1, 5.25, 5.57, 6.20, 7.1p.m.

2. Four years later another BUT has turned at County Gates and has just passed the junction into Seamoor Road on its journey towards the town centre. The route from Westbourne to the Square provided an ideal testing ground for the initial trolleybus experiment of 1933. (G.O.P.Pearce)

3. In this 1958 view 238 (formerly numbered 204) has completed the climb from the Square up Commercial Road and Poole Hill and embarks upon the half mile of level running to Westbourne. In the early years this was not the sole province of service 25; extended versions (21a-24a) of the "main road" routes which normally terminated at the Square also provided a service to County Gates, though in the post-war period this practice gradually died out. (R.F.Mack)

4. Before the days of the present pedestrian-only scheme Commercial Road formed part of a one-way system with Avenue Road. Sunbeam MF2B 262 is just reaching the end of its journey from Charminster Avenue as it climbs up to the terminus at the Triangle. The wires on the right continue on up Poole Hill towards Westbourne. (R.F.Mack)

5. Facilities at the Triangle were improved in 1948 and enabled buses to be parked there during slack periods rather than returning to the central depot. In this 1960 view the park is full to capacity. The Triangle was the terminus for all the "side road" routes, as those services which left the Square via Richmond Hill were known. (J.H.Clifford)

6. The park is rather less congested as one of the 1935 batch of Sunbeam MS2s awaits the return of its crew from a well-earned tea-break. In the 1950s the show alluded to on the small indicator could be at any one of several locations including the Pavilion, Winter Gardens, Palace Court Theatre, Royal Court Theatre, Westover Ice Rink or the Pier Approach Baths. (G.O.P.Pearce)

7. The bunting is out along Avenue Road on 22nd June 1934, the first day of service on route 25. This was an extension towards Boscombe of the highly successful County Gates - Square trial route. In addition to the quartet of experimental vehicles seven new Sunbeam MS2s were available for the first days of the service with a further five joining the fleet within a month.   (G.O.P.Pearce)

8. MF2B 259 is only on its second day in service with the BCT fleet at the time of this photograph in August 1958 and is therefore seen in its original 62 seat condition. The vehicle is adjacent to the feeder cable for this part of the system, the switch box for which can be seen at the foot of the traction standard. The lower indicator still shows the route for the westbound journey and needs to be reset. (G.O.P.Pearce)

9. A 26 bound for Moordown is seen departing its bay in Avenue Road and will shortly select the "express" route for Richmond Hill which avoided negotiating junctions on the circle of wires at the Square. The bus shelters were a post-war innovation based upon the LPTB pattern but mounted at the kerbside. In the background can be seen the Transport Enquiries Office at Fairlight Glen. (G.O.P.Pearce)

October 1949 timetable

SERVICE 26.   Triangle—Square—Moordown
via Cemetery Junction and Winton

WEEKDAYS

		am	am	am	am	am		pm	pm
TRIANGLE	dep.	6 17	6 37	7 0	7 17	7 30	then every	10 59	11 8
Square	„	6 20	6 40	7 2	7 24	7 32	few	11 0	11 10
Winton	„	6 27	6 47	7 9	7 31	7 39	minutes until	11 7	11 17
MOORDOWN	arr.	6 33	6 52	7 15	7 37	7 46		11 14	11 24

		am	am	am	am	am	am	am		pm	pm
MOORDOWN	dep.	6 0	6 20	6 40	6 50	7 0	7 8	then every few minutes until	10 32	10 45
Winton	„	6 6	6 26	6 46	6 56	7 6	7 14		10 38	10 51
Square	„	6 15	6 35	6 54	7 4	7 15	7 22		10 47	11 0
TRIANGLE	arr.	6 17	6 37	6 55	7 5	7 17	7 23		10 48	11 1

SUNDAYS

		am	am	am	am	am		am		pm	pm
TRIANGLE	dep.	5 58	6 53	7 0	8 58	9 47	then every 15 mins. until	11 58	then few mins until	10 27	10 33
Square	„	6 0	6 55	7 2	9 0	9 50		12 5		10 30	10 35
Winton	„	6 6	7 1	7 8	9 6	9 57		12 12		10 37	10 42
MOORDOWN	arr.	6 10	7 5	7 12	9 10	10 5		12 20		10 44	10 49

		am	am	am	am	am	am	am	am	am	am	am	am	am	then	pm	then	pm
M'DOWN	dep.	6 A15	7 B0	7 C13	8 45	9 30	9 45	10 0	10 10	10 18	10 33	10 40	10 48	every 15 mins. until	12 18	every few mins. until	10 15	...
Winton	„	6 33	7 10	...	8 50	9 36	9 51	10 6	10 16	10 24	10 39	10 46	10 54		12 24		10 21	...
Square	„	6 52	7 16	7 28	8 56	9 44	10 0	10 15	10 25	10 33	10 48	10 55	11 3		12 33		10 30	...
TRIANGLE	arr.	6 53	7 17	7 29	8 57	9 45	10 2	10 17	10 27	10 35	10 50	10 57	11 5		12 35		10 33	...

A—via Columbia Rd. and Boscombe.   B—via Ensbury Park Hotel.   C—via Malvern Rd. and Five Ways.

SQUARE - LANSDOWNE

10. In this 1935 view the tram system is still much in evidence with the central shelter the dominant feature of the Square. The conflict of interests is also evident: the trams passing across the Square, the trolleys circulating around it. The story of the tram system in Bournemouth can be discovered in Roy Anderson's volume in the Middleton Press *Tramway Classics* series. (Bournemouth Transport Ltd.)

11. Along with those at the Lansdowne, traffic arrangements at the Square were extensively remodelled in 1947 in order to incorporate a roundabout. However, the clocktower from the former tram shelter was maintained as the central feature. In this view engineering work on the edge of the Lower Pleasure Gardens is going to be a cause of traffic congestion at busy periods. In the left hand corner can be glimpsed part of the roof of the wartime Nissen hut that served as accomodation for bus staff and which was removed in the early 1950s. (Daily Echo, Bournemouth)

12. With the creation of the roundabout at the Square public transport was obliged to make greater use of adjacent areas (such as the Triangle and Avenue Road) as terminal points. On the eastern side Gervis Place became the focal point for the "main road" routes. Four bays were provided to accomodate waiting trolleys. (G.Teasdill)

13. Trolleys arriving at Gervis Place did so by means of alternative routes from the Lansdowne. In this view up Gervis Place towards St. Peter's church the wires coming in via Old Christchurch and Fir Vale Roads can be seen. Trolley 148, on a service from Southbourne, has been routed via Bath and Westover Roads. (R.F.Mack)

14. The alternative route to the Square via Westover Road was provided three years after the original and helped relieve congestion in the narrow confines of Old Christchurch Road. A red blind in the small destination screen gave a clear indication to the passenger of the option being followed. With the Royal Bath Hotel behind him and the final few yards of the journey remaining the driver has already reset the blinds ready for the return trip to Tuckton. (R.F.Mack)

15. The Bournemouth Pier extension was opened on Good Friday 1950. Note that the poles were painted white rather than the usual green in order to appear less obtrusive. Services were always very much at the mercy of seasonal demand and the weather and ran at the discretion of the duty inspector. The wires up Exeter Road to the Square were often useful in helping to marshall stock at peak periods. (S.E.Letts)

June 1956
timetable

SERVICE 38
FISHERMAN'S WALK—BOURNEMOUTH PIER

WEEKDAYS		am	am	am	am	
FISHERMAN'S WALK	dep.	9 26	9 41	9 56	1011	then every 15
BOURNEMOUTH PIER	arr.	9 43	9 51	1013	1028	minutes until

		pm	pm	pm	pm	pm
FISHERMAN'S WALK	dep.	7 11	7 56	8 41	9 26	1011
BOURNEMOUTH PIER	arr.	7 28	8 13	8 58	9 43	1028

		am	am	am	am	
BOURNEMOUTH PIER	dep.	9 46	10 1	1016	1031	then every 15
FISHERMAN'S WALK	arr.	10 8	1023	1038	1053	minutes until

		pm	pm	pm	pm	pm	pm
BOURNEMOUTH PIER	dep.	6 46	7 31	8 16	9 1	9 46	1031
FISHERMAN'S WALK	arr.	7 8	7 53	8 38	9 23	10 8	1053

SUNDAYS				pm	
FISHERMAN'S WALK	... ...	dep.		1226	Then as
BOURNEMOUTH PIER	... ...	arr.		1243	Weekdays

				pm	
BOURNEMOUTH PIER	... ...	dep.		12 1	Then as
FISHERMAN'S WALK	... ...	arr.		1223	Weekdays

Please Note — A curtailed service will be operated on Saturday mornings. This service may be curtailed or withdrawn in the event of inclement weather.

16. In 1958 three MS2s were converted to open top vehicles in order to work the summer-only circular route 39. As well as the obvious modifications to the upper deck the front staircase and exit were removed thereby increasing seating capacity from 56 to 69. Prototype conversion 160 (later to be renumbered 201) is seen undergoing inspection at the Pier in April of that year. The bowler-hatted MOT representative is accompanied by the undertaking's General Manager, Douglas Reakes. (G.O.P.Pearce)

17. The massive bulk of Bath Hill Court forms a backdrop as 271 tackles with customary ease the climb up towards the Lansdowne. Route 38 (formerly 35) was a summer-only service which, from 1961, ran to the turning circle at the end of Carbery Avenue near Tuckton. Prior to this the service terminated at Fisherman's Walk though, for the 1960 season only, it was extended to Christchurch. (P.Thomas)

18. In the last week of trolleybus services in April 1969 MF2B 278 was bedecked in commemorative regalia and makes an attractive sight as it ascends Old Christchurch Road past Horseshoe Common. At the left can be seen part of the turning circle installed during wartime but subsequently used very infrequently. (G.O.P.Pearce)

19. Trolley 273, one of an earlier batch of MF2Bs is pictured near the top of Old Christchurch Road. The wires of the "express" route installed in 1960 for buses bound for Holdenhurst Road have already diverged from the main wires. (R.Sinclair Coll.)

SAFETY FIRST

WAIT

BUS STOP

Until the Bus Stops !

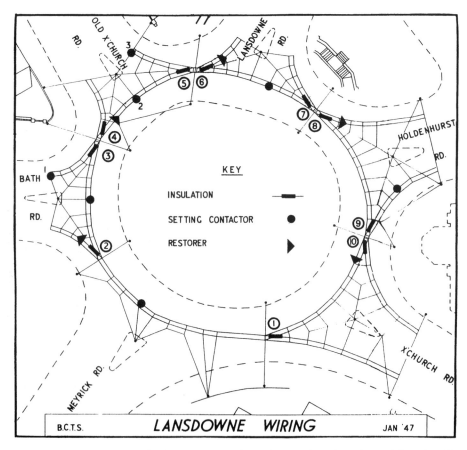

KEY

INSULATION ▬

SETTING CONTACTOR ●

RESTORER ▶

B.C.T.S.   *LANSDOWNE   WIRING*   JAN '47

The 1947 wiring diagram for the new roundabout shows a junction planned for wires for the southern section of Lansdown Road, a line for which powers were never actually sought. However, plans for the loop along Meyrick and Gervis Roads to Bath Hill, for which authority was granted by the 1930 Act, have evidently been abandoned. (D.L.Chalk Coll.)

20. The 1947 roundabout was not the only post-war development at the Lansdowne. The Royal London House, built on the site of the Hotel Metropole which was destroyed by enemy bombs, has not been long completed at the time of this 1958 view. Fortes restaurant has already taken over the ground floor and well-known local estate agents Fox and Son (est. 1868) are responsible for letting the upper accommodation. (G.O.P.Pearce)

21. Trolley 258 was the first of Bourne-mouth's 39 Sunbeam MF2Bs to be received and is seen at the Lansdowne end of Holdenhurst Road during its first few days of service in 1958. Besides the two-axled chassis these buses were distinctive in having a front exit forward of the front axle and parallel with the driver's cab. (G.O.P.Pearce)

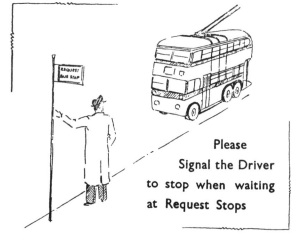

Please
Signal the Driver
to stop when waiting
at Request Stops

22. Route 25 served all of Bournemouth's railway stations at one time, although the 25b service past Pokesdown station en route to Fisherman's Walk operated only from 1938 to 1940. Renumbered BUT 235 passes the Central Goods Depot on its way westwards. The pull for the junction frog for Southcote Road can be seen on the nearest traction standard. (R.F.Mack)

23. This rear-end view of BUT 240, seen at the bus stop on the bridge at Central station, affords an interesting comparison with that of an MS2 (see picture 109). The bodywork is essentially the same but note the varying shape and position of the route indicators, reflectors, registration and fleet number. (G.O.P.Pearce)

24. Trolleybuses were not the only enthusiasm of Gordon Pearce. He also
recorded local railways and motor buses both of which can be seen in this
photograph, taken at the eastern end of the Central station. It is 2.40pm
precisely (we hope) as Merchant Navy class 35015, *Rotterdam Lloyd*,
resplendent in early BR blue glides in with the down Bournemouth Belle.
More views of railways in Bournemouth can be seen in the Middleton Press
Southern Classics. (G.O.P.Pearce)

SAFETY FIRST !

DO NOT BOARD, OR ALIGHT FROM, A MOVING VEHICLE

25. One of British Railways' staff cycles home-
wards after his shift at the depot as 242 passes
the Drill Hall of the Army Cadet headquarters
on the edge of Springbourne. Patrons bound for
the circus in King's Park will still have a walk of
almost half a mile after they have got off at the
Park Gates in Ashley Road.   (R.F.Mack)

26. At Queen's Park Corner MF2B 262 turns into Ashley Road pursued by an interesting queue of vehicles. The Karrier Bantam artic is en route to the BRS depot at Boscombe Station.
(G.O.P.Pearce)

27. From Queen's Park Corner a short spur ran further along Holdenhurst Road to a terminus opposite the former golf pavilion. This spur was used by football traffic generated by nearby Dean Court. Here a line of six Sunbeam MS2s, headed by no.82, await the emergence of the crowds of supporters in March 1935. (G.O.P.Pearce)

28. The turning loop at the golf pavilion terminus can be seen and there is a good view down Holdenhurst Road parallel to where Wessex Way now runs. Until quite late in the system's life plans were afoot to install wires down to the junction with Castle Lane using redundant materials obtained from Ipswich and Brighton. (Bournemouth Passenger Transport Association)

29. On reaching Boscombe buses prepared for the return journey to Westbourne by turning left into Christchurch Road, left again into Portman Road and regaining access to Ashley Road via Gladstone Road. No.259 has just entered the final single line section of Ashley Road as it approaches Christchurch Road. The wires turning out of Gladstone Road can be seen to the right of the vehicle. (G.O.P.Pearce)

Trackless
Rapid acceleration
Odourless
Long life
Loading at kerbside
Easy maintenance
Yields consistent profits
British built
Uses home produced energy
Silent

Acrostic devised by Gordon Pearce for his prize-winning essay *The Future and the Trolleybus* (1956)

30. Two trolleys are seen at rest at the terminus in Portman Road. In front is one of ten BUT 9641Ts that were rebuilt in 1962-63 without the front staircase in order to increase seating capacity. Behind is one of three BUT 9611Ts supplied to Brighton in 1948 and subsequently acquired by Bournemouth in 1959. (R.Sinclair Coll.)

31. Completing the turning procedure at the Boscombe end of route 25 is one of the batch of 48 Sunbeam MS2s delivered between August 1935 and March 1936. No.136 is about to turn right from Gladstone Road into Ashley Road on its return journey to Westbourne. The absence of parked cars compared with today's crowded side roads is noticeable. (G.O.P.Pearce)

CHRISTCHURCH ROAD - IFORD

32. We now return to the Lansdowne to follow the services that travelled along Christchurch Road. One of the ten MF2Bs delivered in the summer of 1959 is seen travelling towards Boscombe. In the distance is the familiar clocktower of the buildings that house the Municipal College and Central Library. (R.F.Mack)

33. Further east along Christchurch Road one of the final batch of MF2Bs is called upon to refute the claim that the trolleybus lacks manoeuvrability. Trolley 299, now preserved by the Irish Transport Museum Society, is easily able to stretch to the far side of the road as it overtakes a coach which has evidently been double-parked for the convenience of patrons of the adjacent hotel. (R.F.Mack)

34. Spring is in the air as two trolleys ascend from Boscombe Gardens towards Lansdowne. No.278 is pictured once again in its commemorative regalia during the final week of trolley services in April 1969. The illuminations for the display were borrowed from the Blackpool tram system. (R.F.Mack)

35. A pair of Sunbeam MS2s pause at Boscombe Arcade on their way eastwards in July 1956 and are seen in a section of Christchurch Road that is now a pedestrian precinct. No.146 has yet to have its wartime chocolate-brown coat of roof paint replaced by peacetime primrose. No.145 had the distinction of being exhibited at the 1935 Commercial Motor Show and was fitted with the prototype large destination screen. Both vehicles have been fitted with modified front route indicators and flush panel by the front staircase. (G.O.P.Pearce)

36. The summer-only circular route 39 was introduced in 1958 and was served by the three open-topped buses converted from Sunbeam MS2s for the purpose. Trolley 200 is seen at Boscombe in the first summer of operation during which the route proceeded in a clockwise direction around the town. The next year the direction of travel was reversed. The service ran only fitfully, being at the mercy of the weather. (G.O.P.Pearce)

37. A little further east travelling in the opposite direction on a 22 the same vehicle is seen in its original state and numbering opposite Crabton Close Road. Patrons of the erstwhile Czech Restaurant were regaled with Viennese zither music whilst they dined. (G.O.P.Pearce)

38. Of the 48 Sunbeam MS2s delivered between August 1935 and March 1936 half were given registration numbers prefaced by the letters BEL and the other half with BRU. One of the former halts at the entrance to Pokesdown depot on its way from Christchurch to the Square. The low facade of the railway station is obscured by the vehicle but the chimney of the local laundry can be espied in the distance. (G.O.P.Pearce)

39. A lengthy queue has formed behind BUT 9641T no.201 which has completed its slow progress to the top of Pokesdown Hill behind auxiliary vehicle LJ1608. This latter vehicle was a former Thornycroft bus converted in 1940 and fitted with special trolley heads in order to lubricate overhead wires. The trolley booms were removed post-war and the vehicle was then used for breakdown work or (as in this instance) delivery of new buses. (G.O.P.Pearce)

40. Trolley 258 has just passed the Harewood Avenue feeder pillar on its way up Pokesdown Hill. On the eastern side of Bournemouth all routes proceeding west from the vicinity of the River Stour are obliged to climb the 100 or so feet up towards the centre of the town. (R.F.Mack)

41. No.172 has reached the foot of Pokesdown Hill and is approaching the Iford roundabout on its way to the route 24 terminus on the far side of Iford Bridge. This vehicle was not allotted a new number in the fleet reorganisation of 1958 and was withdrawn a year later. (G.O.P.Pearce)

42. Buses on service 24 first terminated at a turning circle on the western side of Iford Bridge. This picture, taken on the opening day (25th March 1935) shows the relatively undeveloped nature of the area compared with today. The body of tramcar no.1 served as a waiting room and the barn on the right was used for storing overhead wiring and fittings. The turning circle was removed in 1961 and the site is now a semi-circular garden. (Bournemouth Transport Limited)

43. On the Christchurch side of the bridge a queue of traffic builds up as 259 manoeuvres carefully around sister vehicle 270 which has evidently been struck by technical problems. Route 32 at this time in the 1960s was a service between the Square and Iford via Charminster which terminated either at Iford roundabout, Jumpers Corner or, as on this occasion, somewhere between the two locations. (R.F.Mack)

Iford—Square.

Service No. 24.

IFORD TO SQUARE.
WEEKDAYS—6.34 a.m., 6.49, 7.4, 7.19, 7.34, 7.49, 8.4, then every 8 minutes until 10.52 p.m., 11.8, 11.16 p.m.
SUNDAYS—9.22 a.m., then every 10 minutes until 1.52 p.m., then every 8 minutes until 11.2 p.m.

BOSCOMBE ARCADE TO SQUARE.
WEEKDAYS—6.43 a.m., 6.58, 7.13, 7.28, 7.43, 7.58, 8.13, 8.23, then every 8 minutes until 11.3 p.m., 11.19, 11.27 p.m.
SUNDAYS—9.30 a.m., then every 10 minutes until 2.0 p.m. then every 8 minutes until 11.10 p.m.

SQUARE TO IFORD.
WEEKDAYS—6.56 a.m., 7.11, 7.26, 7.41, 7.56, 8.11, 8.26, 8.36, then every 8 minutes until 11.0 p.m., 11.15, 11.35 p.m.
SUNDAYS—9.42 a.m., then every 10 minutes until 2.12 p.m. then every 8 minutes until 10.52 p.m., 11.15 p.m.

LANSDOWNE TO IFORD.
WEEKDAYS—7.2 a.m., 7.17, 7.32, 7.47, 8.2, 8.17, 8.32, 8.42, then every 8 minutes until 11.6 p.m., 11.21, 11.41 p.m.
SUNDAYS—9.47 a.m., then every 10 minutes until 2.17 p.m., then every 8 minutes until 10.57 p.m., 11.20 p.m.

BOSCOMBE ARCADE TO IFORD.
WEEKDAYS—6.24 a.m., 6.39, 6.54, 7.9, 7.24, 7.39, 7.54, 8.2, 8.9, 8.17, 8.24, 8.34, 8.39, 8.49, then every 8 minutes until 11.13 p.m., 11.28, 11.48 p.m.
SUNDAYS—9.12 a.m., 9.22, 9.32, 9.42, 9.53, then every 10 minutes until 2.23 p.m., then every 8 minutes until 11.3 p.m., 11.26 p.m.

RETURN TICKETS.

The last points at which return tickets will be issued is at:
Boscombe Arcade on the vehicle leaving Iford at 8.36 a.m.
Harewood Avenue   ,,   ,,   Iford at 8.44 a.m.
Horseshoe Common   ,,   ,,   Square at 8.44 a.m.
Boscombe Gardens   ,,   ,,   Square at 8.36 a.m.

For fares see page 37.

Buses travelling via Old Christchurch Road to Square will bear destination boards printed in blue and via Bath Road in Red.

July 1939 timetable

IFORD JUMPERS - CHRISTCHURCH

44. It was not until 1943 that wires were erected across Iford Bridge and along Barrack Road to the junction with Stour Road and (despite opposition from Christchurch Corporation) route 20 came in to being. Trolleys are seen standing in Stourvale Avenue at the new terminus created at Jumpers Corner in 1944 for service 24. (J.H.Meredith)

June 1956 timetable

SERVICES 20, 24. SQUARE — JUMPERS — CHRISTCHURCH
via Lansdowne, Boscombe Gardens, Boscombe, Pokesdown. Iford,
WEEKDAYS

		am	am	am	am	am	am	am	am	am	am	am	am	am	am	am	am
SQUARE	dep.	—	—	6 56	7 10	7 25	7 43	7 53	8 08	8 13	8 23	8 28	8 38	8 43	8 53	9 4	9 17
Boscombe	,,	6 34	6 58	7 09	7 21	7 38	7 56	8 06	8 21	8 25	8 35	8 40	8 50	8 55	9 5	9 16	9 29
Jumper's Corner	,	6 43	7 06	7 15	7 29	7 47	8 06	8 16	8 30	8 35	8 45	8 50	9 0	9 5	9 15	9 27	9 40
CHRISTCHURCH	arr.	6 50	7 13	—	7 36	7 55	8 14	—	8 38	—	—	—	9 8	—	9 23	—	9 48

				pm	pm
SQUARE	Dep.	Then every 10 minutes		10 57	11 07
Boscombe	,,	to Jumpers Corner		11 10	11 10
Jumpers Corner	,,	and every 20 minutes to		11 20	11 30
CHRISTCHURCH	Arr.	Christchurch until		11 28	—

		am	am	am	am	am	am	am	am	am	am	am	am	am	am	am	am
CHRISTCHURCH	dep.	—	—	6 54	—	7 17	—	7 40	—	—	8 0	—	8 15	—	—	—	8 45
Jumpers Corner	,,	6 20	6 43	7 2	7 17	7 25	7 40	7 48	7 58	8 3	8 8	8 18	8 23	8 33	8 38	8 45	8 53
SQUARE	arr.	6 42	7 4	7 25	7 40	7 48	8 3	8 11	8 21	8 25	8 30	8 40	8 45	8 55	9 0	9 7	9 15

		am	am	am			pm	pm	pm
CHRISTCHURCH	dep.	—	—	9 13	then every 20 mins. from Christ-		10 53	11x08	11x28
Jumpers Corner	,,	9 1	9 11	9 21	church and every 10 mins. from		11 01	—	—
SQUARE	arr.	9 24	9 34	9 44	Jumpers Corner until		11 24	—	—

45. MF2B no.264 is seen in Barrack Road opposite the former site of the Military Engineering Experimental Establishment. The array of Bailey Bridges and other assorted ironmongery that could be seen was always a fascinating part of a visit to this area. (R.F.Mack)

46. At the junction with Stour Road the route joined the route 21 wires past Christchurch Station and then into Bargates. Trolley 284, making the return journey towards Bournemouth, will shortly cross the railway bridge before passing MEXE. (R.Sinclair Coll.)

47. When, in 1954, a roundabout was installed between Bargates and the High Street in preparation for the proposed Christchurch bypass, BCT found that they had no authority to reroute the trolley wires around it. For a year until the Bournemouth Corporation (Trolley Vehicles) Order Confirmation Act 1955 was passed buses travelled, courtesy of a special traffic light system, the wrong way across the northern part of the roundabout. In this 1960s picture a 21 is seen leaving the southern portion of the roundabout en route for Bargates. (R.Sinclair Coll.)

48. The view along Christchurch High Street from the upper deck of a westbound bus shows an in-coming 21 proceeding towards the terminus. Access to the turntable in Church Street was governed by an indicator light placed strategically on one of the traction standards in the High Street. (P.Thomas)

49. The tower of the magnificent Norman priory church can be seen behind one of the final batch of MF2Bs as it cautiously emerges from the alley that leads to the turntable. The nearside trolley boom is about to pass the contact for the light in the High Street which will then indicate that the facility is vacant. (P.Thomas)

50. Although the route to Christchurch was opened on 8th April 1936, it was not for another two months that the famous turntable was installed at a cost of £380 in the former coach yard of the Dolphin Hotel. Note that this bus is destined for Westbourne on an extension of route 21 and the service number will therefore bear an "a" suffix. (D.Conrad)

51. The turntable was not, as is often maintained, unique in the annals of trolleybus lore. Huddersfield had one on a precipitous outcrop of their system from which a vehicle once toppled. There was also one at the Bilston depot of the Wolverhampton system. The conductor is in the process of removing the booms from the wires prior to turning the vehicle. (P.Thomas)

52. From time to time the turntable needed to be taken out of service for maintenance. On such occasions buses on routes 20 and 21 had to be turned in Church Street using a T-pole. This device enabled current to be taken from the wires and applied to the lowered trolley booms in order to effect the turning procedure.
(Daily Echo, Bournemouth)

53. Returning to Pokesdown we now follow the lines through Southbourne. In 1955 the route down to Cranleigh Road is still numbered 22b as Sunbeam MS2 165 pauses by the fire station. Due to the expansion of the fleet during 1950-51 extra storage for trolleybuses was provided temporarily at the rear of the nearby depot and to which access was gained opposite this spot in Seabourne Road.
(G.O.P.Pearce)

BOURNEMOUTH CORPORATION TRANSPORT SERVICES

ALTERATION TO SERVICE NUMBERS

Commencing Thursday 1st March, 1956, revised service numbers will be introduced on the undermentioned routes:—

OLD NUMBER		NEW NUMBER
3A	SQUARE — ENSBURY PARK — REDHILL DRIVE	2
3B	SQUARE — ENSBURY PARK — LEYBOURNE AVENUE — WEST HOWE	6
7A	BOSCOMBE — ENSBURY PARK — LEYBOURNE AVENUE	8
9A	SQUARE — WALLISDOWN — MACLEAN ROAD	10
10 ✷	BOSCOMBE — BOSCOMBE PIER	16
22B	SQUARE — CRANLEIGH ROAD — TUCKTON BRIDGE	23
23	SQUARE — FISHERMAN'S WALK	37
25A	WESTBOURNE — QUEEN'S PARK — ASHLEY ROAD	25
26A	SQUARE — LAWFORD ROAD — WEST WAY	27
27	SQUARE — CENTRAL STATION — MOORDOWN	34
28A	SQUARE — CASTLE LANE — WEST WAY	29
29	SQUARE — FIVE WAYS — MALVERN ROAD	35
30A	SQUARE — ENSBURY PARK ROAD — COLUMBIA ROAD	31
31	SQUARE — STROUDEN PARK — IFORD	32
34 ✷	COLUMBIA ROAD — ENSBURY PARK — CENTRAL STATION — B'MOUTH PIER	36
35 ✷	FISHERMAN'S WALK — BOURNEMOUTH PIER	38

✷ SUMMER SERVICES

Transport Offices,
99/101, Southcote Road,
BOURNEMOUTH.   Telephone 1701.

W. D. REAKES,
GENERAL MANAGER.

54. A view of the crossroads at Fisherman's Walk from the upper deck of an eastbound bus. The weather is fine for a ride on the open-top trolley which is en route from Carbery Avenue to the Pier. Up until 1960 the eastern terminus for this service was in the area just off to the right behind the bus. (P.Thomas)

55. In 1956 route 22b was renumbered 23. At Fisherman's Walk in 1963 two trolleys are ready to descend Beaufort Road on the route to Tuckton. No.214 was loaned to Wolverhampton during the War and was withdrawn in the same year as this photo. However, trolley 235 has three more years of service still to give. (G.O.P.Pearce)

56. From January to March 1968 Southbourne Grove was the subject of an unpopular experiment in traffic control. Only trolleybuses were permitted to pass along its entire length, through traffic of other types being redirected along other roads in the vicinity. The nature of the restriction to traffic is apparent as two trolleys prepare to pass each other. (G.Teasdill)

57. MF2Bs are seen crossing at Carbery Row in Southbourne Road. BCT long resisted the need to raise revenue by sullying the external appeareance of trolleybuses with advertising material. However, economic pressures eventually prevailed and for the last two years of their existence trolleys were obliged to carry advertisements. (J.Clifford)

58. Erection of the wires between Pokesdown and Tuckton proceeded in stages during 1935 and 1936 and reached Southbourne Crossroads in December 1935. The turning circle created in the area where St.Catherine's Road, the Coast Road and the Overcliff Drive converge was used until 1946 as the terminus for route 22 and thereafter for occasional short or special workings. Having used the circle an MF2B is seen re-emerging into Belle Vue Road. (R.Sinclair Coll.)

July 1939 fare table.

FARE TABLE.

SERVICE No. 21, 22, 23, WESTBOURNE—CHRISTCHURCH.

Transfer Fare, Fisherman's Walk—Iford 2d.

Special Fares, Westbourne—Bournemouth Arcade 1½d.
Fisherman's Walk—Guildhill Rd. (11) 1½d.

Westbourne (1) S R W	Surrey Road (2) S R W	Square (3) S R W	Lansdowne (4) S R W	Boscombe Arcade (5) S R W	Parkwood Road (7) S R W	Fisherman's Walk (9) S R W	Cross Roads (10) S R W	Tuckton Bridge West (12) S R W	Tuckton Bridge E. (13) S R W	Christchurch (15)
1 - -										
1 - -	1 - -									
2 2 1	2 2 1	1 - -								
3 3 1½	3 3 1½	2 2 1	1 - -							
3½ - -	3½ - -	2½ - -	1½ - -	- - -						
4 4 2	4 4 2	3 3 1½	2 2 1	1 - -	- - -					
5 5 2½	5 5 2½	4 4 2	3 3 1½	2 2 1	1½ 2 1	1 - -				
6 6 3	6 6 3	5 5 2½	4 4 2	3 3 1½	2½ 3 1½	2 2 1	1 - -			
6½ - -	6½ - -	5½ - -	4½ - -	3½ - -	3 - -	2½ - -	1½ - -	- - -		
7 8 4	7 8 4	6 7 3½	5 6 3	4 5 2½	4 5 2½	3½ 4 2	2½ 3 1½	1½ - -	1 - -	Christchurch (15)

S.—SINGLE.   R.—RETURN.   W.—WORKMEN'S

The fare from the Pavilion, Westover Road, is a ½d. more than the fare charged from the Square.

59. About half of the system's junction frogs were automatically operated. As the driver of 270 approaches Tuckton roundabout he will have applied power as he passed beneath the contact in order to activate the solenoid for Tuckton Road. An indicator light on the right hand traction standard will confirm that he has selected the correct route. The route number will be changed since the vehicle now returns to Fisherman's Walk via Cranleigh Road as a 23. The driver of 298 following behind on route 21 will coast beneath the contact in order to proceed straight on towards Christchurch. (R.J.Harley Coll.)

60. The elegance of Tuckton Bridge and the way in which the trolley gantries are integrated into the structure via the buttresses can be fully appreciated in this view. Sunbeam MS2 217 (formerly 119) is en route from Christchurch to the Square. (J.S.King)

61. The photographer has positioned himself by the site of the former toll kiosk in order to gain this picture of trolley 259 proceeding in the opposite direction. Until 1942 passengers paid a halfpenny surcharge on buses crossing the bridge. The kiosk finally closed on 1st October 1943. Note the sign prohibiting more than one trolleybus on the bridge at a time. (P.Thomas)

62. We return to Fisherman's Walk via the Cranleigh Road to Beresford Road lines installed in 1948. At the foot of Carbery Avenue, near the Tuckton end, a turning circle was provided, being in a less constricted venue than at Tuckton itself. The summer-only service 38 from Bournemouth Pier used this as a turning point from 1961 onwards. An MF2B on service 23 has just passed the circle and has already changed the number to 22 in readiness for the return journey up Belle Vue Road. (J.Clifford)

WHEN   WAITING   AT   REQUEST   STOPS

‖

PLEASE SIGNAL

THE   DRIVER   TO   STOP

63. In March 1957 a party of enthusiasts on a Sunday afternoon tour of the complete trolleybus system pose for a group portrait at the Carbery Avenue turning circle. On the far left of the back row is Deputy Chief Inspector William Biddlecombe, test driver of the first trolleys to arrive in the town and the trainer of no less than 1,671 drivers. At the opposite end stands Gordon Pearce, who was responsible for many of the pictures in this book. In front of him, aged six, stands the present author.
(G.O.P.Pearce)

64. Further along Cranleigh Road we note that the driver of this bus has, as yet, failed to change the number from 22 to 22b (as route 23 was known prior to 1956). Eager to ride on one of the October 1934 batch of Sunbeam MS2s a lady passenger leaps on to the rear platform. (G.O.P.Pearce)

65. At the corner where Cranleigh Road meets Beaufort Road another MS2 is pictured within a few days of its withdrawal from service in 1959. Behind can be seen Stourfield School where the present author received his early education. (G.O.P.Pearce)

October 1949 timetable

SERVICE 22b. Westbourne—Square—Tuckton Bridge
via Fisherman's Walk, Beaufort Road and Cranleigh Road
WEEKDAYS

		am	am	am	am	am	am	am	am	am	am	am	am	am
WESTBOURNE	dep.	...	...	...	...	7 50	...	...	...	...	8 42	...	9 11	9 34
SQUARE	,,	...	7 28	...	7 48	7 58	8	8 18	8 28	8 38	8 48	8 58	9 18	9 42
Fisherman's Walk	,,	7 37	7 47	7 57	8	8 17	8 27	8 37	8 47	8 57	9	9 17	9 25	9 37	10 1
Cranleigh Road	,,	7 42	7 52	8	2 8 12	8 22	8 32	8 42	8 52	9	2 9 12	9 22	9 31	9 43	10 7
TUCKTON BRIDGE	,,	7 46	7 56	8	6 8 16	8 26	8 36	8 46	8 56	9	6 9 16	9 26	9 36	9 48	1012

		am	am	am	am	am	am	am	pm	pm	pm(	pm	pm	pm	pm	pm
WESTBOURNE	dep.	9 58	1022	1046	1110	1134	1158	1222	1246	1 10	1 34	1 58	2 22	2 46	3 10
SQUARE	,,	10 6	1030	1054	1118	1142	12 6	1230	1254	1 18	1 42	2 16	2 30	2 54	3 18
Fisherman's Walk	,,	1025	1049	1113	1137	12 1	1225	1249	1 13	1 37	2 1	2 25	2 49	3 13	3 37
Cranleigh Road	,,	1031	1055	1119	1143	12 7	1231	1255	1 19	1 43	2 7	2 31	2 55	3 19	3 43
TUCKTON BRIDGE	arr.	1036	11 0	1124	1148	1212	1236	1 0	1 24	1 48	2 12	2 36	3 0	3 24	3 48

		pm	pm	pm	pm	pm	pm	pm	pm	pm	pm	pm			pm
WESTBOURNE	dep.	3 34	3 58	4 22	4 46	5 10	5 34	5 58	6 22	6 46	7 9	7 27	then		1047
SQUARE	,,	3 42	4 6	4 30	4 54	5 18	5 42	6 6	6 30	6 54	7 15	7 35	every		1055
Fisherman's Walk	,,	4 1	4 25	4 49	5 13	5 37	6 1	6 25	6 49	7 13	7 34	7 54	20		1114
Cranleigh Road	,,	4 7	4 31	4 55	5 19	5 43	6 7	6 31	6 55	7 19	7 40	8 0	mins.		1120
TUCKTON BRIDGE	arr.	4 12	4 36	5 0	5 24	5 48	6 12	6 36	7 0	7 24	7 45	8 5	until		1125

Between 9-25 a.m. and 7-54 p.m. additional Buses operate between Fisherman's Walk and Tuckton Bridge, giving a 12 minute frequency between these points.

		am	am	am	am	am		am(	am(	am	am	am	am
TUCKTON BRIDGE	dep.	7 0	7 14	7 28	7 40	7 49	then	8 59	9 9	9 21	9 45	10 9	1033	1047
Cranleigh Road	,,	7 4	7 18	7 32	7 44	7 54	every	9 4	9 14	9 26	9 50	1014	1038	11 2
Fisherman's Walk	,,	7 9	7 23	7 37	7 49	7 59	10	9 9	9 20	9 32	9 56	1020	1044	11 8
SQUARE	,,	7 28	7 42	7 55	8	8 18	mins.	9 29	...	9 51	1015	1039	11 3	1127
WESTBOURNE	arr.	...	...	...	...	...	until			9 58	1022	1046	1110	1134

		am	pm	pm	pm	pm	pm	pm	pm	pm	pm	pm	pm	pm	pm
TUCKTON BRIDGE	dep.	1121	1145	12 9	1233	1257	1 21	1 45	2 9	2 33	2 57	3 21	3 45	4 9	4 33
Cranleigh Road	,,	1126	1150	1214	1238	1 2	1 26	1 50	2 14	2 38	3 2	3 26	3 50	4 14	4 38
Fisherman's Walk	,,	1132	1156	1220	1244	1 8	1 32	1 56	2 20	2 44	3 8	3 32	3 45	4 20	4 44
SQUARE	,,	1151	1215	1239	1 3	1 27	1 51	2 15	2 39	3 3	3 27	3 51	4 15	4 39	5 3
WESTBOURNE	arr.	1158	1222	1246	1 10	1 34	1 58	2 22	2 46	3 10	3 34	3 58	4 12	4 46	5 10

		pm	pm	pm	pm	pm	pm	pm	pm			pm	pm
TUCKTON BRIDGE	dep.	4 57	5 21	5 45	6 9	6 33	6 57	7 21	7 50	then every		1030	1050
Cranleigh Road	,	5 2	5 26	5 50	6 14	6 38	7 2	7 26	7 55	20 minutes		1035	1055
Fisherman's Walk	,,	5 8	5 32	5 56	6 20	6 44	7 8	7 32	8 1	until		1041	11 1
SQUARE	,,	5 27	5 51	6 15	6 39	7 3	7 27	7 51	8 20			11 0	1120
WESTBOURNE	arr.	5 34	5 58	6 22	6 46	7 10	7 34	7 58	8 27			11 7	...

Between 9-9 a.m. and 7-33 p.m. additional Buses operate between Fisherman's Walk and Tuckton Bridge, giving a 12 minute frequency between these points.
(On the inward journey Buses travel via Bath and Westover Roads, and on the outward journey via Old Christchurch Road)

66. It is early morning on the inaugural day of route 22b on 11th August 1948. At the top of Beaufort Road the crew of trolley 128 seem able to pose in front of their vehicle without fear of disrupting traffic. The wires diverging to the right formed part of a circle around Southbourne and Parkwood Roads which enabled local short workings to turn. The anticlockwise direction of travel was reversed for the duration of a short-lived one-way scheme in 1967-68. (G.O.P.Pearce)

RICHMOND HILL and WIMBORNE ROAD

67. Richmond Hill was the only exit from the Square for the "side road" routes although in the mid 1950s there was a proposal to create a relief route along Bourne Avenue and up Braidley Road to Wimborne Road. In late 1935 the tramlines are still in place, but the trams and the single overhead wires have gone. The view looks across the Square to the spire of St.Andrew's Church and the entrance to the erstwhile Hants and Dorset bus station, destroyed by fire and now the site of a car park. (Bournemouth Transport Limited)

68. Almost a quarter of a century later the scene up the hill shows representatives of later generations of vehicles. On the 1 in 8 gradient the power and smooth acceleration of the trolleybus showed marked superiority over combustion-engined types. Safe braking was given high priority: on the BUT 9641Ts, for instance, the coasting brake restricted the vehicle to 7mph down a hill of this nature. A safety run-back brake limiting speed to half mph was also installed. (G.O.P.Pearce)

69. The crowds of pedestrians are well advised to LOOK RIGHT as a representative of the "silent service" creeps on to the Square. The pedestrians have now taken over completely since the bottom of Richmond Hill has been paved for their exclusive use. After the renumbering from 26a, service 27 continued briefly in the summer of 1956 on a reciprocal basis with route 29 (formerly 28a). Thereafter, the number disappeared from the timetables and was used to indicate workings through to Mallard Road depot. (A.J.Douglas)

70. A view from an upper window of the Echo offices affords a good chance to study the roof detail of trolleybuses descending Richmond Hill in the rush hour. The walkway along the centre of the roof provided a safe foothold for maintenance purposes. The upper rear window hinged downwards and was able to bear the weight of someone fitting a new carbon insert into the trolley head. (Daily Echo, Bournemouth)

71. The potential for development at the top of Richmond Hill is already being advertised in 1964 in a scene that predates the Wessex Way interchange and the Zurich tower. (P.Thomas)

72. Trolley 268 speeds towards Cemetery Junction on a 31 bound via Ensbury Park for Columbia Road. From thence it will return as a 30 via Talbot Village. Routes along Wimborne Road conveyed supporters to county cricket at Dean Park or, as in this case, to championship tennis at the West Hants club. (R.J.Harley Coll.)

73. As 153 pulls away from the lights at Cemetery Junction we have a view back along Charminster Road. There is also an opportunity to note the rival cultural delights offered at the Pavilion and the Winter Gardens. The Bournemouth Municipal Orchestra did not gain its present title of Symphony Orchestra until 1958. (W.J.Haynes)

28 29	Triangle—Bournemouth Square—Five Ways—Broadway / Triangle—Bournemouth Square—Five Ways—West Way	28 29

WEEKDAYS

	am	am	am	am	am	am	am	Then at the following mins. past each hour		until	pm
Triangle ... dep	6 28	7 16	7 58	8 15	...	8 43	8 52	22	44 52		6 22
Square (Avenue Road) ,,	6 30	7 17	8 00	8 17	...	8 47	8 56	26	48 56		6 26
King's Road ... ,,	6 37	7 24	8 07	8 24		8 54	9 03	33	55 03		6 33
Five Ways ... ,,	6 41	7 28	8 11	8 28	8 53	8 58	9 07	37	59 07		6 37
Broadway ... arr	6 45	7 32	8 15	8 32	8 57	9 02	9 11	41	03 11		6 41
West Way ... arr		7 34	——	8 34	8 59		9 13	43	—— 13		6 43

	pm	pm	pm	pm	pm	Then at the following mins. past each hour until		pm	pm	pm	pm
Triangle ... dep	6 44	6 52	7 04	7 24	7 48		04 24 44	1004	1024	1044	1104
Square (Avenue Road) ,,	6 48	6 56	7 08	7 28	7 48		08 28 48	1008	1028	1048	1108
King's Road ... ,,	6 55	7 03	7 15	7 35	7 55		15 35 55	1015	1035	1055	1115
Five Ways ... ,,	6 59	7 07	7 19	7 39	7 59		19 39 59	1019	1039	1059	1119
Broadway ... arr	7 03	7 11	7 23	7 43	8 03		23 43 03	1023	1043	1103	1123
West Way ... arr	——	7 13	——	7 45			45			1045	

	am	am	am	am	am	am	am	am	am	Then at the following mins. past each hour		am	am	am	am
West Way ... dep	...	...	7 12	...	7 39	7 54			8 25	8 39			8 54	...
Broadway ... ,,	6 05	6 45	7 00	7 14	7 26	7 41	7 56	8 16	8 27	8 41	8 48	8 56	9 04
Five Ways ... ,,	6 09	6 49	7 04	7 18	7 30	7 45	8 00	8 20	8 31	8 45	8 52	9 00	9 08
King's Road ... ,,	6 13	6 53	7 08	7 22	7 34	7 49	8 04	8 24	8 35	8 49	8 56	9 04	9 12
Square ... ,,	6 20	7 00	7 15	7 29	7 41	7 56	8 11	8 31	8 42	8 56	9 03	9 11	9 19
Triangle ... arr	6 21	7 01	7 16	7 30	7 42	7 57	8 12		8 43	8 57	9 04	9 12	9 20

	Then at the following mins. past each hour until		pm	pm	pm	pm	pm	Then at the following mins. past each hour		pm
West Way ... dep	22 52		...	6 22	6 52	...	7 48		... 48	1048
Broadway ... ,,	24 54 04		6 24	6 54	7 04	7 30	7 50		10 30 50	1050
Five Ways ... ,,	28 58 08		6 28	6 58	7 08	7 34	7 54		14 34 54	1054
King's Road ... ,,	32 02 12		6 32	7 02	7 12	7 38	7 58		18 38 58	1058
Square ... ,,	39 09 19		6 39	7 09	7 19	7 45	8 05		25 45 05	1105
Triangle ... arr	40 10 20		6 40	7 10	7 20	7 46	8 06		26 46 06	1106

September 1958 timetable.

74. BUT 257 (formerly 223) crosses Cemetery Junction en route for the Square. In this photograph we can see the lights controlling the traffic leaving Lansdowne Road but notice that the wires that used to take trolleybuses on services 34 and 36 along to St.Paul's Road and the Central Station have been removed. (R.F.Mack)

34	Lansdowne—Winton—Moordown—West Way—Broadway													34

WEEKDAYS														
	am	am	am	am	am	am	am	am	am	am	am	am	am	am
Lansdowne (Hold'rst Rd.) dep	6 30	6 55	7 22	7 37	7 48	7 58	8 07	8 22	8 36	9 04	9 34	1004		
Banks, Winton ... ... „	6 38	7 02	7 29	7 44	7 56	8 06	8 14	8 29	8 44	9 12	9 42	1012		
Moordown (P.O.) ... ... „	6 44	7 08	7 35	7 50	8 02	8 12	8 21	8 36	8 50	9 18	9 48	1018		
Lawford Road ... ... „	6 46	7 10	7 37	7 52	8 04	8 14	8 23	8 38	8 52	9 20	9 50	1020		
West Way ... ... „	—	7 12	7 39	7 54			8 25		8 54	9 22	9 52	1022		
Broadway... ... ... arr	...	7 14	7 41	7 56	...	...	8 27	...	8 56	9 24	9 54	1024		

	am	am	am				pm	pm	pm	pm	pm			
Lansdowne (Hold'rst Rd.) dep	1034	1104	1134		04	34	5 04	5 34	6 04	6 34	7 04			
Banks, Winton ... ... „	1042	1112	1142	Then at the following mins. past each hour	12	42	until	5 12	5 42	6 12	6 42	7 12		
Moordown (P.O.) ... ... „	1048	1118	1148		18	48		5 18	5 48	6 18	6 48	7 18		
Lawford Road ... ... „	1050	1120	1150		20	50		5 20	5 50	6 20	6 50	7 20		
West Way ... ... „	1052	1122	1152		22	52		5 22	5 52	6 22	6 52	7 22		
Broadway... ... ... arr	1054	1124	1154		24	54		5 24	5 54	6 24	6 54	7 24		

	am	am		am	am	am	am			am	am	am		
Broadway... ... ... dep	5 59	6 29	...	7 02	7 17	7 32	7 47	...	...	8 32	...	9 11		
West Way ... ... „	6 01	6 31	...	7 04	7 19	7 34	7 49	...	...	8 34	...	9 13		
Lawford Road ... ... „	6 03	6 33	6 50	7 06	7 21	7 36	7 51	8 06	8 20	8 36	8 43	9 15		
Moordown (P.O.) ... ... „	6 05	6 35	6 52	7 08	7 23	7 38	7 53	8 08	8 22	8 38	8 45	9 17		
Banks, Winton ... ... „	6 11	6 41	6 58	7 14	7 29	7 44	7 59	8 14	8 28	8 44	8 51	9 23		
Lansdowne (Hold'rst Rd.) arr	6 19	6 49	7 06	7 22	7 37	7 52	8 07	8 22	8 36	8 52	8 59	9 31		

	am	am	am	am	am				pm	pm	pm	pm		
Broadway... ... ... dep	9 41	1011	1041	1111	1141		11 41		5 41	6 11	6 41	7 11		
West Way ... ... „	9 43	1013	1043	1113	1143	Then at the following mins. past each hour	13 43	until	5 43	6 13	6 43	7 13		
Lawford Road ... ... „	9 45	1015	1045	1115	1145		15 45		5 45	6 15	6 45	7 15		
Moordown (P.O.) ... ... „	9 47	1017	1047	1117	1147		17 47		5 47	6 17	6 47	7 17		
Banks, Winton ... ... „	9 53	1023	1053	1123	1153		23 53		5 53	6 23	6 53	7 23		
Lansdowne (Hold'rst Rd.) arr	1001	1031	1101	1131	1201		31 01		6 01	6 31	7 01	7 31		

Additional journeys from Lansdowne to Columbia Road at 4.50 p.m., 5.20 p.m., 5.50 p.m.														

September
1958
timetable.

WINTON, WALLISDOWN and MOORDOWN

75. At Winton Banks trolleys on short local workings could turn, in much the same way as service 25 at Boscombe and service 23 at Fisherman's Walk, via a circuit of side roads. No.272 and one of the ex Brighton and Hove BUT 9611Ts are seen in Crimea Road with the Wimborne Road frontage of Lloyd's Bank in the background. The 1938 Transport Act made provision for a route to be constructed along Alma and Richmond Park Roads to Holdenhurst Road. (M.J.C.Dare)

76. Lloyds Bank is now seen on the left, as a 30 bus stands at the start of Talbot Road ready for the journey up towards Wallisdown. Trolley 122 is sporting one of the redesigned route indicators that were fitted to Sunbeam MS2s in the early 1950s. (G.O.P.Pearce)

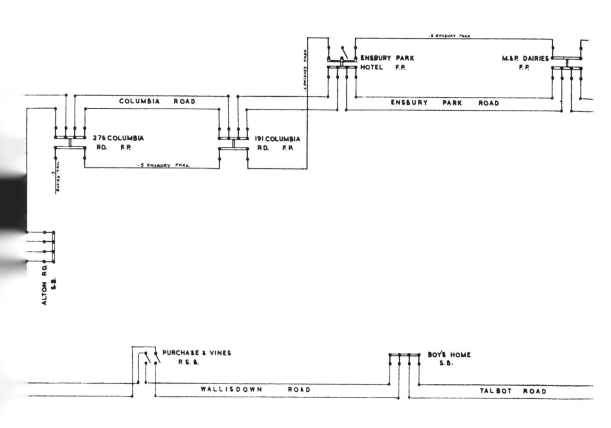

Pages 38 & 39 of the 1965 Positive Feeder System diagram show the location of Feeder Pillars (F.P.) and Switch Boxes (S.B.) for this part of the system. P.S.B. indicates a pole-mounted switch box. Positive underground cables connecting the feeder pillars are shown in red on the original. (R.Sinclair Coll.)

77. The wires reached up past Talbot Village to the junction of Kinson and Columbia Roads in April 1938, those coming from the opposite direction via Ensbury Park Road not being installed until a year later. Until then buses arriving at the terminus were obliged to make a tight turning manoeuvre via the access road in front of the small parade of shops. On the first day of operations on service 30 no.102 has turned and is ready for the return journey. This route was the first on which slipper heads on the trolley booms replaced wheel-type collectors. (G.O.P.Pearce)

July 1939 fare table.

SERVICES 30 and 30a

SQUARE, WINTON, WALLISDOWN, ENSBURY PARK, WINTON, SQUARE (and vice versa).

SPECIAL FARES.

Hendford Road (16)   Brassey Road (10) ... 1d.
Hendford Road (16)   Banks, Winton (8) ... 1½d.

S. R. W.																	
Square (3)																	
1 - -	Cemetery Junction (6)																
1½ - -	1 - -	Banks, Winton (8)															
2 2 1	1 - -	1 - -	Heathwood Road (12)														
2½ 3 1½	2 2 1	1 - -	1 S.	Boys' Home (9)													
3 - -	2½ - -	1½ - -	1½	1 - -	Talbot Village Church (10)												
3½ - -	3 - -	2 - -	2	1½ - -	1 - -	Wallisdown Liberal Club (11)											
3½ 4 2	3 3 1½	2 2 1	-	2 - -	1 - -	1 - -	Columbia Road (17)										
4½ - -	4 - -	3 - -		3 3 1½	2 - -	1½ - -	1 - -	Ensbury Park Hotel (15)									
5½ - -	5 - -	4 - -	-	4 - -	3 - -	2 - -	1½ - -	1 - -	Brassey Road (10)								
5½ - -	5 - -	4 - -	-	4 - -	3 3 1½	2½ - -	2 - -	1 - -	1 S.	Peter's Hill (9)							
5½ - -	5 - -	4 - -	-	4 - -	3 - -	2½ - -	2 2 1	1½ - -	1	1 - -	Banks, Winton (8)						
6½ - -	6 - -	5 - -	-	5 - -	4 - -	3 - -	3 3 1½	2 2 1	1½ 1 - -	1	Cemetery Junc. (6)						
7 - -	6½ - -	5½ - -	-	5½ - -	4½ - -	3½ 4 2	3½ 4 2	3 3 1½	2½ 2 2 1	1½ 1	Square (3)						

S.—SINGLE.   R.—RETURN.   W.—WORKMEN'S.

78. The popularity of the bus that was so spectacularly decorated for the 1937 Coronation (see 111 & 112) encouraged a similar venture the following year, when 152 was again bedecked in honour of the Royal Counties Show and is pictured at the Columbia Road terminus. The crew includes the doyen of Bournemouth trolley drivers, William Biddlecombe (centre). (G.O.P.Pearce)

79. The lines connecting Columbia Road to Ensbury Park Road and through to Winton were completed just before the outbreak of the War. The route was originally numbered 30a, but in the 1956 reorganisation of route numbers was allotted 31. Like several other pairs of routes in the Bournemouth system, services 30 and 31 were reciprocal. No.264 started from the Triangle as a 30 and on its return journey as a 31 is approaching the crossroads formed by Columbia, Ensbury Park and Boundary Roads and Redhill Drive, now the site of a gyratory system. (R.F.Mack)

80. Having turned out of Ensbury Park Road and into Wimborne Road trolley 295 is at the crest of Peter's Hill and has passed the former fire station on the left. On this dull day passengers will appreciate better the benefits of the lighter decor and the flourescent lighting with which the final batch of MF2Bs were fitted. (R.F.Mack)

81. Also returning to the Square along Wimborne Road and pictured at the point where Waitrose and W.H.Smith now stand is BUT 141. This vehicle is not so far from the site of its collision with 212 at Stokewood Road in December 1950. This bus would have started from the Triangle as a 28a bound for Charminster changing its identity to 26a at the end of West Way in Castle Lane. In the 1956 reorganisation these two services were allocated the numbers 29 and 27 respectively. (R.J.Harley Coll.)

82. At the northern end of Wimborne Road trolleys travelling towards Iford were routed down Lawford Road, which also acted as a terminal point for certain services. Only buses bound in the opposite direction proceeded, as in this picture, via the junction of Wimborne Road and Castle Lane. At one time the undertaking entertained considerable plans to expand the system towards Bear Cross with feeder lines into the rapidly growing suburbs of Kinson, West Howe and Northbourne. (W.J.Haynes)

October 1951 timetable.

27 **Square—Lansdowne—Moordown** **27**
via Central Station and Winton

From SQUARE—Mondays to Fridays—7.12 a.m., 7.22, 7.37, 7.52, then every few minutes until 9.38 a.m., then every 10 minutes until 7.38 p.m., 7.50, then every 15 minutes until 10.50 p.m., 11.2.

Saturdays—As Mondays to Fridays until 9.38 a.m., then every 10 minutes until 10.48 p.m., 11.2.

Sundays—8.0 a.m., 9.50, then every 15 minutes until 2.5 p.m., 2.18, then every 10 minutes until 7.38 p.m., 7.50, then every 15 minutes until 10.35 p.m.

From MOORDOWN—Mondays to Fridays—6X5 a.m., 6X35, 6.47, 7.0, 7X8, 7.15, 7X22, 7.30, then every few minutes until 9.17 a.m., then every 10 minutes until 7.17 p.m., 7.29, then every 15 minutes until 10.29 p.m., 10.41.

Saturdays—As Mondays to Fridays until 9.17 a.m., then every 10 minutes until 10.27 p.m., 10X36, 10.42.

Sundays—7.35 a.m., 8X25, 8.35, 9.29, then every 15 minutes until 1.44 p.m., 1.57, then every 10 minutes until 7.17 p.m., 7.29, then every 15 minutes until 10.14 p.m.

X—to Lansdowne only.

83. MF2B 298 has turned the corner into Wimborne Road and passes Westover Motors on its way up towards Moordown. With the 1956 renumbering from 27 to 34 the route of this service was altered to start at West Way and terminate at the Lansdowne. Apart from the rush-hour 36 (formerly 34) and the summer-only circular tour this was the only regular trolley service along Lansdowne and St.Paul's Roads. That section of wiring was the first to be dismantled and little, if any, photographic evidence is known to exist. (G.O.P.Pearce)

A further extract from the 1965 Positive Feeder System diagram shows the layout at this most northerly point of the system. Details include the location of feeder pillars, a switch box, the jumper bars across insulation points near the Lawford Road junction and the Luckham Road reverser. (R.Sinclair Coll.).

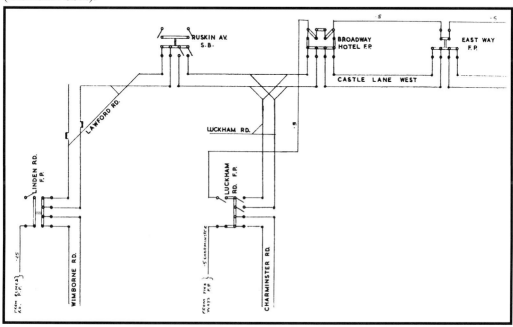

CHARMINSTER and CASTLE LANE

84. Charminster Road runs roughly parallel to Wimborne Road and was served by a similar selection of services. Service 28 ran along Charminster Road to Broadway Hotel at the junction with Castle Lane. BUT 242, on the return journey to the Triangle, is climbing up from Five Ways towards the Alma Road traffic lights, passing between St.Alban's C of E church and the R C Church of the Assumption as it does so. (R.F.Mack)

85. Another BUT is pictured descending to Five Ways on its way back to the centre of the town. Service 29 (formerly 28a) was an extension of 28 that terminated at the end of West Way in Castle Lane. From the autumn of 1956 it operated on a reciprocal basis with service 34 which had replaced 27 (formerly 26a) in that role. (J.M.Llewellyn / Omnicolour)

86. From Five Ways a short spur ran up Charminster Avenue as far as the junction with Malvern Road. The 1938 Act provided for an extension through to Moordown and joining Wimborne Road by the former bus depot there. Trolley 300 is seen completing the reversing manoeuvre by St. Walburga's school. Route 35 was identified as 29 prior to the 1956 reorganisation. (R.F.Mack)

SERVICE 35.—(formerly Service 29)—TRIANGLE—SQUARE—MALVERN RD.
via Cemetery Junction, Charminster Road and Five Ways

WEEKDAYS

		am	am	am	am	am	am	pm	pm		pm	pm	pm
TRIANGLE ... ... dep.		6 55	7 32	7 48	8 03	8 21	8 33	8 53	9 5	then	9 35	9 59	1029
Square ... ... ,,		6 57	7 34	7 50	8 05	8 23	8 35	8 55	9 9	every	9 39	10 3	1033
King's Road ... ... ,,		7 04	7 41	7 58	8 13	8 31	8 43	9 3	9 17	30	9 47	1011	1041
Five Ways ... ... ,,		7 07	7 44	8 00	8 15	8 33	8 45	9 5	9 19	mins.	9 49	1013	1043
MALVERN ROAD ... ... arr.		7 09	7 48	8 04	8 19	8 37	8 48	9 8	9 23	until	9 53	1017	1047

		am	am	am	am	am	am	am	pm	pm		pm	pm	pm
MALVERN ROAD ... ... dep.		7 10	7 33	7 48	8 5	8 20	8 38	8 48	9 8	9 26	then	9 56	1018	1048
Five Ways ... ... ,,		7 13	7 36	7 51	8 08	8 23	8 41	8 51	9 11	9 29	every 30	9 59	1021	1051
Square ... ... ,,		7 24	7 47	8 02	8 19	8 34	8 52	9 02	9 22	9 40	mins.	1010	1032	11 1
TRIANGLE ... ... arr.		7 25	7 48	8 3	8 20	8 35	8 53	9 3	9 23	9 41	until	1011	1033	11 2

SUNDAYS

		pm			pm
TRIANGLE ... ... dep.		2 5	then		10 5
Square ... ... ,,		2 9	every		10 9
King's Road ... ... ,,		2 17	30		1017
Five Ways ... ... ,,		2 19	mins.		1019
MALVERN ROAD ... ... arr.		2 23	until		1023

		pm	pm	then	pm	pm
MALVERN ROAD ... dep.		—	2 26	every	9 56	1023
Five Ways ... ... ,,		7 20	2 29	30	9 59	1026
Square ... ... ,,		7 28	2 40	mins.	1010	1037
TRIANGLE ... ... arr.		7 29	2 41	until	1011	1058

June 1956 timetable.

October 1951
timetable.

87. Just before Charminster Road reached Castle Lane a reversing triangle was located at the entrance to Luckham Road to enable buses terminating at Broadway Hotel and those serving schools situated nearby to reverse direction. The wiring layout can be seen as trolley 216 proceeds towards the Square on the first day of the short-lived 31/32 circular service in October 1951. There is evidently some confusion since service 31 was intended to operate in a clockwise direction. (G.O.P.Pearce)

88. The route numbers 31 and 32 were reallocated in 1953. The number 31 was allotted to the Triangle - Iford service which was further renumbered 32 in 1956. It is in this latter guise that 118 is seen proceeding along Castle Lane towards Strouden Park in 1958. (G.O.P.Pearce)

October 1953 timetable.

SERVICE 31. Square—Strouden Park—Iford
via Charminster Road.

WEEKDAYS

		am	am	am	am	pm	pm	pm	pm	pm	pm	pm	pm	pm	pm	pm	pm		pm	pm
SQUARE	... dep.	8 35	9 50	10 50	11 50	12 50	1 50	2 30	2 50	3 30	3 50	4 30	4 50	5 5	5 30	5 50	6 30	6 55	then hourly until	9 55	10 55
King's Road	... ,,	8 41	9 56	10 56	11 56	12 56	1 56	2 36	2 56	3 36	3 56	4 36	4 56	5 11	5 36	5 56	6 36	7 1		10 1	11 1
Strouden	... ,,	8 53	10 8	11 8	12 8	1 8	2 8	2 48	3 8	3 48	4 8	4 48	5 8	5 20	5 48	6 8	6 48	7 13		10 13	11 13
Holdenhurst Rd.	... ,,	8 55	10 10	11 10	12 10	1 10	2 10	2 50	3 10	3 50	4 10	4 50	5 10	5 23	5 50	6 10	6 50	7 15		10 15	11 15
IFORD	... arr.	8 59	10 14	11 14	12 14	1 14	2 14	—	3 14	—	4 14	—	5 14	5 25	—	6 14	—	7 19		10 19	—

		am	am	am	am	am	pm	pm	pm	pm	pm	pm	pm	pm	pm	pm	pm		pm	pm
IFORD	... dep.	—	8 16	—	9 42	10 42	11 42	12 42	1 42	—	2 42	—	3 42	—	4 42	—	5 25	5 42	—	6,42	7 48 8 48 9 48 10 44
Holdenhurst Rd.	... ,,	8 5	8 20	8 30	9 46	10 46	11 46	12 46	1 46	2 2	2 46	3 2	3 46	4 2	4 46	5 2	5 27	5 46	6 2	6 46	7 52 8 52 9 52 10 48
Strouden	... ,,	8 7	8 22	8 32	9 48	10 48	11 48	12 48	1 48	2 2	2 48	3 2	3 48	4 2	4 48	5 2	5 30	5 48	6 2	6 48	7 54 8 54 9 54 10 50
King's Road	... ,,	8 17	8 32	8 42	9 58	10 58	11 58	12 58	1 58	2 18	2 58	3 18	3 58	4 18	4 58	5 18	5 38	5 58	6 18	6 58	8 4 9 4 10 4 11 0
SQUARE	... arr.	8 25	8 40	8 50	10 6	11 6	12 6	1 6	2 6	2 26	3 6	3 26	4 6	4 26	5 6	5 26	5 46	6 6	6 26	7 6	8 11 2 9 11 2 10 12 11 8

SUNDAYS

				am	am	am	pm	pm	pm		pm	pm	pm	pm
SQUARE	...	...	... dep.	—	10 8	11 8	12 25	1 17	1 50	then hourly until	6 55	7 55	8 55	9 55
King's Road	...	...	... ,,	—	10 14	11 14	12 31	1 23	1 56		7 1	8 1	9 1	10 1
Strouden	...	...	... ,,	—	10 23	11 25	12 42	1 34	2 8		7 13	8 13	9 13	10 13
Holdenhurst Road	...	...	... ,,	9 26	10 25	11 28	12 45	1 37	2 10		7 15	8 15	9 15	10 15
IFORD	...	...	... arr.	9 30	10 29	11 32	12 49	1 41	2 14		7 19	8 19	9 19	10 19

				am	am	am	pm	pm	pm		pm	pm	pm	pm
IFORD	...	...	... dep.	9 30	10 30	11 35	12 50	1 42		then hourly until	6 42	7 48	8 48	9 48	10 44
Holdenhurst Road	...	...	... ,,	9 34	10 34	11 39	12 54	1 46			6 46	7 52	8 52	9 52	10 48
Strouden	...	...	... ,,	9 36	10 36	11 41	12 56	1 48			6 48	7 54	8 54	9 54	10 50
King's Road	...	...	... ,,	9 46	10 46	11 51	1 6	1 58			6 58	8 4	9 4	10 4	—
SQUARE	...	...	... arr.	9 54	10 54	11 59	1 14	2 6			7 6	8 12	9 12	10 12	—

89. A companion picture to 87. This no.32 bus is seen travelling in a clockwise direction - counter to that intended - on the first day of the service in October 1951. In the background can be seen the modest crossroads formed by the intersection of Castle Lane and Holdenhurst Road - a very different scene compared with today's busy flyover! (G.O.P.Pearce)

October 1953 timetable.

SERVICE 33.   Square—Winton—Moordown—Strouden Park—Iford

WEEKDAYS

			am	am	am	am		pm	pm		pm	pm
SQUARE ...	...	dep.	6 38	—		9 10		6 10	7 15		10 15	10 45
Winton ...	...	"	6 44	A	8 12	9 17	then	6 17	7 22	then	10 22	10 52
Moordown ...	...	"	6 50	8 0	8 18	9 24	hourly	6 24	7 29	hourly	10 29	10 59
Strouden Park ...	...	"	6 57	8 10	8 27	9 33	until	6 33	7 38	until	10 38	11 6
Holdenhurst Road ...	...	"	6 59	8 13	8 30	9 35		6 35	7 40		10 40	11 8
IFORD ...	...	arr.	7 2	8 16	—	9 39		6 39	7 44		10 44	11 12

			am	am	am		pm	pm		pm	pm	
IFORD ...	...	dep.	7 5	—	9 17		6 17	7 26		10 26	11 12	....
Holdenhurst Road ...	...	"	7 8	7 55	9 21	then	6 21	7 30	then	10 30	11 16	...
Strouden Park ...	...	"	7 10	7 57	9 23	hourly	6 23	7 32	hourly	10 32	11 18	...
Moordown ...	...	"	7 17	8 5	9 32	until	6 32	7 41	until	10 41	—	...
Winton ...	...	"	7 22	8 11	9 38		6 38	7 47		10 47	—	...
SQUARE ...	...	arr.	—	—	9 47		6 47	7 55		10 55	—	...

SUNDAYS

			pm		pm	pm		pm	pm
SQUARE ...	...	dep.	2 10		6 10	7 15		10 15	10 30
Winton ...	...	"	2 17	then	6 17	7 22	then	10 22	10 37
Moordown ...	...	"	2 24	hourly	6 24	7 29	hourly	10 29	10 44
Strouden Park ...	...	"	2 33	until	6 33	7 38	until	10 38	10 53
Holdenhurst Road ...	...	"	2 35		6 35	7 40		10 40	10 55
IFORD ...	...	arr.	2 39		6 39	7 44		10 44	—

			pm		pm	pm		pm	pm
IFORD ...	...	dep.	2 17		6 17	7 26		9 26	10 30
Holdenhurst Road ...	...	"	2 21	then	6 21	7 30	then	9 30	10 34
Strouden Park ...	...	"	2 23	hourly	6 23	7 32	hourly	9 32	10 36
Moordown ...	...	"	2 32	until	6 32	7 39	until	9 39	—
Winton ...	...	"	2 38		6 38	7 45		9 45	—
SQUARE ...	...	arr.	2 47		6 47	7 54		9 54	—

A—Through Bus to the Square via Boscombe

90. Five months before its withdrawal from service trolley 127 is pictured in July 1955 in the sylvan surroundings of the turning circle provided at Strouden Park in 1953. This was situated adjacent to the crossroads and was removed in 1962 when a roundabout was built. Although principally an Iford service at this time a number of 31 buses were scheduled to turn at this point. (G.O.P.Pearce)

91. Care was evidently taken to preserve well established trees when the roundabout was built, although all was later swept away by the Wessex Way - Ringwood Spur Road flyover that now dominates this site. No.246 (formerly 212) makes its way towards Mallard Road as part of the final procession on 20th April 1969. This vehicle was exhibited at the Commercial Motor Show in September 1950 but was damaged three months later in the collision with 141. Although officially withdrawn from service in 1966 it was preserved by the Bournemouth Passenger Transport Association. (R.Sinclair Coll.)

92. At Iford the Castle Lane wires met the Christchurch route in an impressive triangular junction. The route along Castle Lane took some time to construct, much to the frustration of the growing local population, and was served initially (and, as we have seen, somewhat confusingly) by a circular service. On October 15th 1951 no.219 continues upon its erroneous way to the Square via Boscombe rather than Charminster. (G.O.P.Pearce)

93. The junction was upgraded to a roundabout in 1956 and the wiring modified accordingly. In July 1958 one of the corporation's gardens staff appears concerned for the well-being of his barrow as one of the newly acquired Sunbeam MF2Bs, out on driver training, cautiously makes the circuit. (G.O.P.Pearce)

94. To complete the survey of routes covered by Bournemouth trolleybuses we catch a glimpse of one of a number of Sunbeams that did wartime service for the LPTB in Ilford. Other trolleys spent the war years in such diverse locations as Wolverhampton, Walsall, Newcastle, Llanelli and South Shields. For security reasons the words BOURNEMOUTH CORPORATION would have been removed from the side of the vehicle in its home town and one assumes that, in this particular case, they have been allowed to remain in order to disorientate an invading force. (A.B.Cross)

DEPOTS

95. The central depot at Southcote Road dates from the beginning of the century when the tramway system was developed. Until 1955 the undertaking generated much of the electricity for the system from its own power station whose chimney and cooling towers stood prominently at the western end of the site. Coal arrived via the No.10 siding of the adjacent railway goods yard. In this wartime view a number of trolleys have been dispersed in St. Clement's Road as a precaution against air attack on the depot. (G.O.P.Pearce)

96. Access to the depot from the Central station end was along Southcote Road and from the Boscombe end via Palmerstone and St.Clement's Roads. No public trolley service ran along these roads and a set of triple wires was provided for vehicles to run to and from the depot. These can be clearly seen in this picture of trolleys awaiting attention beside the former power house. (Phil Picken)

97. A view into the eastern end of the site taken from the corner of Vale Road and St Clement's Road. On 16th June 1934 trolley 72, sporting the gleaming white roof that was characteristic of the first batch of MS2s, is a very new arrival at the depot. In the early years the trolley heads were equipped with wheel type collectors. The limited information given by the single line destination indicators was augmented by boards on the side of the vehicle.
(G.O.P.Pearce)

98. An array of Sunbeam MS2s is seen within the the depot precincts in early 1951. Enlarged route indicators soon replaced the original type and were supplemented with the additional information given by the small indicator over the nearside cab window. Later on during the fifties some older vehicles (such as No.144, nearest the camera) acquired the arrangement of indicators that was standard on the new BUTs. Southcote Road depot closed to buses in 1965 but continues to be used by the Borough Engineer's department. (G.O.P.Pearce)

99. From 1906 the undertaking also maintained two smaller depots. The northern part of the system was served by a depot at Moordown situated on the corner of Wimborne and Malvern Roads. At the end of 1953, with the completion of the first phase of building at Mallard Road, it was closed and subsequently leased to the GPO Telephones department. Route 27 buses are here seen being prepared for use on the penultimate day of operations at the depot. (D.Conrad)

100. Pokesdown Depot served the eastern part of the system and was in use up until the end of 1967, the declining fleet of trolleys from thenceforth being housed exclusively in the recently extended facilities at Mallard Road. Being situated on a main road (as at Moordown) meant that the manoeuvring of vehicles in and out of the depot required careful supervision. Inspector Wally Hiscock is pictured directing operations on the last day. (D.L.Chalk)

101. The final major extension of the system along Castle Lane was tied in with the start of work on the prestigious new bus depot at Mallard Road near Strouden Park. An ambitious scheme, it involved the construction of the largest span of pre-stressed concrete in the country at that time. The first phase was not complete until 1953 though, in this 1951 view, some use is already being made of the garage facilities to store superannuated stock whilst construction continues. (G.O.P.Pearce)

102. The garage was intended to accomodate 99 vehicles. Here representatives of the three principal generations of Bournemouth trolleys pose at the entrance. No.277 was one of the first batch of MF2Bs to be delivered and is seen in company with a 1950 BUT and one of the MS2s delivered in early 1935. The open top MS2 was originally numbered 112 and acquired the fleet number 202 upon its conversion in 1958. (G.O.P.Pearce Coll.)

103. The interior of the maintenance block shows the network of inspection pits in full use with diesel and trolley buses sharing the facilities. The fully tiled inspection pits were illuminated by flourescent lighting. Galleries facilitated the maintenance of electrical equipment. (Bournemouth Transport Limited)

STOCK

For the initial 1933 experimental route four vehicles were hired and were eventually purchased outright for a total of £7,345.

104. Sunbeam MS2, no.68 was originally supplied with rear entrance/exit only, but is here seen at a later date by the Southcote Road power house in modified condition with the front exit/rear entrance arrangement that became standard on all Bournemouth trolleybuses. The unique front end of the Weymann bodywork distinguished this vehicle from the other Sunbeams that were subsequently supplied to the undertaking. (D.Conrad)

105. Two vehicles were obtained from the Associated Equipment Company and were fitted with English Electric bodywork. The three axle model 661T, no.69, was converted to a motor bus in 1936 and is seen in that condition at Boscombe Pier. It is ironic that a former trolley should eventually visit a location that was the subject of one of the very first "trackless" schemes proposed for Bournemouth. This vehicle was sold in 1950 and ended its days as a mobile ladies convenience in Southend! (G.O.P.Pearce)

106. Sister vehicle 70 was a two-axle model 633T which was also later converted to petrol running and is seen here in its original state in the Square. It seems oddly prophetic that the manufacturer should have supplied these two vehicles with dummy radiators! (D.L.Chalk Coll.)

107. The novelty among the four vehicles was 71, the unique single-deck Thornycroft which was fitted with Brush motor and bodywork. This 32 seater was originally supplied in blue and was soon nicknamed "Bluebird" - as much for its speed as for its colour. It was repainted in standard livery and was eventually sold to South Shields Corporation in 1943. (R.Sinclair Coll.)

Of the experimental vehicles the Sunbeam was selected in 1934 to act as the prototype of the Bourne-
mouth fleet. Over the next two years the undertaking acquired the largest fleet of trolleys purchased
from a single manufacturer and which numbered 103 vehicles in all.
SUNBEAM MS2, H31/25D.
AEL 400-411, nos 72-83, delivered June-July 1934, withdrawn 1952-57
ALJ 60-65, nos 84-89, some renumbered 205-208, delivered October 1934, withdrawn 1957-63
ALJ 964-999, nos 90-125, some renumbered 209-218, delivered Feb-June 1935, withdrawn 1951-63
BEL 811-834 & BRU 1 -24, nos 126-173, some renumbered 219-233, delivered Aug 1935-March 1936, withdrawn 1951-64
Nos. 112,157 & 160 converted to open top (69 seats) in 1958 and renumbered 200-202

108. At the date of this photograph taken at the Triangle in July 1951 this
representative of the six English-Electric bodied MS2s had covered 540,000
miles and had been loaned to the LPTB between 1940 and 1942. The rest of
the Sunbeam fleet were equipped with Park Royal bodies. (G.O.P.Pearce)

109. The Shamrock and Rambler man looks on as we take the opportunity to study the rear-end details of trolley 130 waiting outside the former branch of W.H.Smith at Fisherman's Walk. The turning loop situated on the south side of the cross roads was the terminus for the peak-hours only service 23 and, until 1959, the summer-only service 35. In 1956 these were renumbered 37 and 38 respectively. (G.O.P.Pearce)

110. No.148 models wartime livery in St. Clement's Road. Hooded headlamps, chocolate-brown roof and white flashes on the wheel arches are all evident. Various experiments to mask light from the windows were tried at the start of the war and included painting them blue. The words BOURNE-MOUTH CORPORATION were also removed from the sides, never to be reinstated. (G.O.P.Pearce)

111. A dramatic head-on view of 152 at Pokesdown decorated in celebration of the 1937 Coronation of King George VI. (G.O.P.Pearce)

112. Some 1100 light bulbs were employed in the decorations and at night the Coronation bus was a spectacular sight with varying effects controlled by a rotary changer.
(Bournemouth Passenger Transport Association)

113. Trolley 202 has completed its delivery journey from Addlestone to Southcote Road and is seen at rest inside the depot. The front panel, removed for access to the towing point, has not yet been replaced. (G.O.P.Pearce)

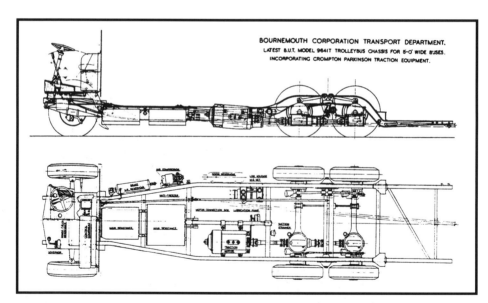

BOURNEMOUTH CORPORATION TRANSPORT DEPARTMENT.
LATEST B.U.T. MODEL 9641T TROLLEYBUS CHASSIS FOR 8'-0" WIDE BUSES.
INCORPORATING CROMPTON PARKINSON TRACTION EQUIPMENT.

In 1950 the undertaking purchased a fleet of luxurious new vehicles in order to meet the demands of an expanding network and to replace the oldest trolleys.
BRITISH UNITED TRACTION 9641T. H31/25D, some later converted to H39/29D without front staircase.
KLJ 334-357, nos.200-223, all renumbered 234-257, delivered Sept.-Nov.1950, withdrawn 1965-1966

114. The generous spacing, high quality of furnishing and luxurious decor with which the BUT fleet were fitted by Metro Cammell Weymann are apparent in this interior view of the upper deck.
(G.O.P.Pearce Coll.)

115. The view into the driver's cab shows the essential controls. Remember, the power pedal is on the LEFT, the brake pedal on the RIGHT of the steering column!
(G.O.P.Pearce Coll.)

In 1959 Bournemouth acquired seven BUT 9611T two-axle vehicles at a cost of £250 each from the redundant Brighton Corporation and Brighton, Hove and District Omnibus Co. fleets.
BRITISH UNITED TRACTION, 9611T. H30/26D
HUF 45-48, nos 288-291, built 1947; DNJ 992-994, nos 292-294, built 1948; withdrawn 1965.

116. One of the ex-Brighton Corporation vehicles is seen at the Triangle in September 1963. These compact and speedy trolleybuses with seating for 56 did not have the front exit common to the vehicles that were built specifically for BCT and were found to be of greatest use in rush-hour traffic. (G.O.P.Pearce)

117. Unlike many other similar undertakings, Bournemouth Corporation Transport erected and maintained all its own wiring, and did so to a very high standard. The 32,000 or so poles and their attendant wiring were serviced over the years with the aid of a succession of tower wagons, the oldest of which were converted from Tilling-Stevens buses. A single purpose-built Bedford wagon was purchased in 1937. After the war this was joined by two wagons converted from AEC 661 buses that once belonged to Huddersfield, one of which is seen here in action at the Triangle. (A.B.Cross)

118. A study of the numbering and the Corporation coat of arms on the rear of a BUT. The motto "beauty and good health" is apt not only for the town but for this elegant and environmentally friendly method of transport. (G.O.P.Pearce)

BCT took delivery of 39 two-axle Sunbeam MF2Bs between 1959 and 1962. One of the intended final batch of ten was never delivered, having been destroyed in a fire at Weymann's body works. All vehicles had a fleet number identical to the registration and survived until the withdrawal of trolley services in 1969.
SUNBEAM MF2B. H35/28D (nos.258-287), H37/28D (nos.295-303)
WRU 258-277, delivered July 1958-January 1959
YLJ 278-287, delivered July-September 1959
295-303 LJ, delivered July-October 1962.

119. Although not the last in its fleet numbering, 301 was the final trolleybus to be supplied to a British operator. Fittingly, it was allotted the place of honour as the last vehicle in the farewell procession from the Pier to Mallard Road on Sunday 20th April 1969. The bus sets off with well-known local personality and England mascot, Ken Bailey, in his customary John Bull outfit in hot pursuit. (Daily Echo, Bournemouth)

FINALE

120. A view, from close to where the Bournemouth International Centre now stands, of the procession of trolleys assembled at the Pier. Only the final four vehicles carrying the VIPs travelled all the way to the Christchurch turntable before returning to Mallard Road. The rest of the parade turned left at the junction of Stour and Barrack Roads. Much has changed since this picture was taken. The Pier Approach baths have disappeared, and the Hants & Dorset bus company, whose depot is seen in the background, is no more. Pedestrians no longer require a zebra crossing in order to get to the Pier since the road is now carried above their heads by a flyover. However, it is ironic to note that, almost thirty years on, the trolleybus has been seriously reconsidered as the best method of moving people around Bournemouth's busy town centre. (G.O.P.Pearce)

No **736**

BOURNEMOUTH CORPORATION TRANSPORT

SOUVENIR TICKET

issued on the last journey by

TROLLEYBUS

from Bournemouth Pier to Christchurch
and Mallard Road Depot – fare 3/–

SUNDAY, 20th APRIL, 1969

Middleton Press

Easebourne Lane, Midhurst, W Sussex. GU29 9AZ Tel: 01730 813169 Fax: 01730 812601
Email: enquiries@middletonpress.fsnet.co.uk *If books are not available from your
local transport stockist, order direct with cheque, Visa or Mastercard, post free UK.*

BRANCH LINES
Branch Line to Allhallows
Branch Line to Alton
Branch Lines around Ascot
Branch Line to Ashburton
Branch Lines around Bodmin
Branch Line to Bude
Branch Lines around Canterbury
Branch Lines around Chard & Yeovil
Branch Line to Cheddar
Branch Lines around Cromer
Branch Line to the Derwent Valley
Branch Lines to East Grinstead
Branch Lines of East London
Branch Lines to Effingham Junction
Branch Lines around Exmouth
Branch Lines to Falmouth, Helston & St. Ives
Branch Line to Fairford
Branch Lines around Gosport
Branch Line to Hayling
Branch Lines to Henley, Windsor & Marlow
Branch Line to Hawkhurst
Branch Line to Ilfracombe
Branch Line to Kingsbridge
Branch Line to Kingswear
Branch Line to Lambourn
Branch Lines to Launceston & Princetown
Branch Lines to Longmoor
Branch Line to Looe
Branch Line to Lyme Regis
Branch Line to Lynton
Branch Lines around March
Branch Lines around Midhurst
Branch Line to Minehead
Branch Line to Moretonhampstead
Branch Lines to Newport (IOW)
Branch Line to Newquay
Branch Lines around North Woolwich
Branch Line to Padstow
Branch Lines around Plymouth
Branch Lines to Princes Risborough
Branch Lines to Seaton and Sidmouth
Branch Lines around Sheerness
Branch Line to Shrewsbury
Branch Line to Swanage *updated*
Branch Line to Tenterden
Branch Lines around Tiverton
Branch Lines to Torrington
Branch Lines to Tunbridge Wells
Branch Line to Upwell
Branch Lines of West London
Branch Lines of West Wiltshire
Branch Lines around Weymouth
Branch Lines around Wimborne
Branch Lines around Wisbech

NARROW GAUGE
Branch Line to Lynton
Branch Lines around Portmadoc 1923-46
Branch Lines around Porthmadog 1954-94
Branch Line to Southwold
Douglas to Port Erin
Douglas to Peel
Kent Narrow Gauge
Northern France Narrow Gauge
Romneyrail
Southern France Narrow Gauge
Sussex Narrow Gauge
Surrey Narrow Gauge
Swiss Narrow Gauge
Two-Foot Gauge Survivors
Vivarais Narrow Gauge

SOUTH COAST RAILWAYS
Ashford to Dover
Bournemouth to Weymouth
Brighton to Worthing
Eastbourne to Hastings
Hastings to Ashford
Portsmouth to Southampton
Ryde to Ventnor
Southampton to Bournemouth

SOUTHERN MAIN LINES
Basingstoke to Salisbury
Bromley South to Rochester
Crawley to Littlehampton
Dartford to Sittingbourne
East Croydon to Three Bridges
Epsom to Horsham
Exeter to Barnstaple
Exeter to Tavistock
Faversham to Dover
London Bridge to East Croydon
Orpington to Tonbridge
Tonbridge to Hastings
Salisbury to Yeovil
Sittingbourne to Ramsgate
Swanley to Ashford
Tavistock to Plymouth
Three Bridges to Brighton
Victoria to Bromley South
Victoria to East Croydon
Waterloo to Windsor
Waterloo to Woking
Woking to Portsmouth
Woking to Southampton
Yeovil to Exeter

EASTERN MAIN LINES
Barking to Southend
Ely to Kings Lynn
Ely to Norwich
Fenchurch Street to Barking
Hitchin to Peterborough
Ilford to Shenfield
Ipswich to Saxmundham
Liverpool Street to Ilford
Saxmundham to Yarmouth
Tilbury Loop

WESTERN MAIN LINES
Bristol to Taunton
Didcot to Banbury
Didcot to Swindon
Ealing to Slough
Exeter to Newton Abbot
Newton Abbot to Plymouth
Newbury to Westbury
Paddington to Ealing
Paddington to Princes Risborough
Plymouth to St. Austell
Princes Risborough to Banbury
Reading to Didcot
Slough to Newbury
St. Austell to Penzance
Swindon to Bristol
Taunton to Exeter
Westbury to Taunton

MIDLAND MAIN LINES
St. Albans to Bedford
Euston to Harrow & Wealdstone
St. Pancras to St. Albans

COUNTRY RAILWAY ROUTES
Abergavenny to Merthyr
Andover to Southampton
Bath to Evercreech Junction
Bath Green Park to Bristol
Burnham to Evercreech Junction
Cheltenham to Andover
Croydon to East Grinstead
Didcot to Winchester
East Kent Light Railway
Fareham to Salisbury
Frome to Bristol
Guildford to Redhill
Reading to Basingstoke
Reading to Guildford
Redhill to Ashford
Salisbury to Westbury
Stratford upon Avon to Cheltenham
Strood to Paddock Wood
Taunton to Barnstaple
Wenford Bridge to Fowey
Westbury to Bath
Woking to Alton
Yeovil to Dorchester

GREAT RAILWAY ERAS
Ashford from Steam to Eurostar
Clapham Junction 50 years of change
Festiniog in the Fifties
Festiniog in the Sixties
Festiniog 50 years of enterprise
Isle of Wight Lines 50 years of change
Railways to Victory 1944-46
Return to Blaenau 1970-82
SECR Centenary album
Talyllyn 50 years of change
Wareham to Swanage 50 years of change
Yeovil 50 years of change

LONDON SUBURBAN RAILWAYS
Caterham and Tattenham Corner
Charing Cross to Dartford
Clapham Jn. to Beckenham Jn.
Crystal Palace (HL) & Catford Loop
East London Line
Finsbury Park to Alexandra Palace
Holbourn Viaduct to Lewisham
Kingston and Hounslow Loops
Lewisham to Dartford
Lines around Wimbledon
Liverpool Street to Chingford
London Bridge to Addiscombe
Mitcham Junction Lines
North London Line
South London Line
West Croydon to Epsom
West London Line
Willesden Junction to Richmond
Wimbledon to Beckenham
Wimbledon to Epsom

STEAMING THROUGH
Steaming through Cornwall
Steaming through the Isle of Wight
Steaming through Kent
Steaming through West Hants

TRAMWAY CLASSICS
Aldgate & Stepney Tramways
Barnet & Finchley Tramways
Bath Tramways
Brighton's Tramways
Bristol's Tramways
Burton & Ashby Tramways
Camberwell & W.Norwood Tramways
Clapham & Streatham Tramways
Croydon's Tramways
Dover's Tramways
East Ham & West Ham Tramways
Edgware and Willesden Tramways
Eltham & Woolwich Tramways
Embankment & Waterloo Tramways
Exeter & Taunton Tramways
Fulwell - Home to Trams, Trolleys and Buses
Great Yarmouth Tramways
Greenwich & Dartford Tramways
Hammersmith & Hounslow Tramways
Hampstead & Highgate Tramways
Hastings Tramways
Holborn & Finsbury Tramways
Ilford & Barking Tramways
Kingston & Wimbledon Tramways
Lewisham & Catford Tramways
Liverpool Tramways 1. Eastern Routes
Liverpool Tramways 2. Southern Routes
Liverpool Tramways 3. Northern Routes
Maidstone & Chatham Tramways
Margate to Ramsgate
North Kent Tramways
Norwich Tramways
Reading Tramways
Seaton & Eastbourne Tramways
Shepherds Bush & Uxbridge Tramways
Southend-on-sea Tramways
South London Line Tramways 1903-33
Southwark & Deptford Tramways
Stamford Hill Tramways
Twickenham & Kingston Tramways
Victoria & Lambeth Tramways
Waltham Cross & Edmonton Tramways
Walthamstow & Leyton Tramways
Wandsworth & Battersea Tramways

TROLLEYBUS CLASSICS
Croydon Trolleybuses
Derby Trolleybuses
Hastings Trolleybuses
Huddersfield Trolleybuses
Maidstone Trolleybuses
Portsmouth Trolleybuses
Reading Trolleybuses
Woolwich & Dartford Trolleybuses

WATERWAY ALBUMS
Kent and East Sussex Waterways
London to Portsmouth Waterway
West Sussex Waterways

MILITARY BOOKS
Battle over Portsmouth
Battle over Sussex 1940
Blitz over Sussex 1941-42
Bombers over Sussex 1943-45
Bognor at War
Military Defence of West Sussex
Military Signals from the South Coast
Secret Sussex Resistance
Surrey Home Guard

OTHER RAILWAY BOOKS
Index to all Middleton Press stations
Industrial Railways of the South-East
South Eastern & Chatham Railways
London Chatham & Dover Railway
London Termini - Past and Proposed
War on the Line (SR 1939-45)

BIOGRAPHY
Garraway Father & Son